LATIN FOR PEOPLE | LATINA PRO POPULO

LATINA
PRO
POPULO

ALEXANDRI HUMEZ

PARVULA FUSCAQUE SOCIETAS

BOSTONIA | TORONTO

LATIN
FOR
PEOPLE

NICHOLAS HUMEZ

LITTLE, BROWN AND COMPANY
BOSTON | TORONTO

FIRST EDITION

T 04/76

The illustration on page 88 is reproduced by permission of the Harvard College Library.

Library of Congress Cataloging in Publication Data

Humez, Alexander.
  Latin for people — Latina pro populo.

  1. Latin language — Grammar — 1950–
I. Humez, Nicholas, joint author. II. Title.
III. Title: Latina pro populo.
PA2087.H82   478'.2'421   76-2436
ISBN 0-316-38150-0

Published simultaneously in Canada
by Little, Brown & Company (Canada) Limited

PRINTED IN THE UNITED STATES OF AMERICA

For Hilda Allen,

DULCE LUMEN LUXQUE FACTI

CONTENTS

Comfortable Words
(and Others)

There is really no fast and easy way to learn a language: the feast is simply too vast and too varied to be completely digested in anything less than a full lifetime, even by the most efficient metabolism. On the other hand, it isn't always necessary to make away with the whole spread to feel some measure of pleasant satisfaction. Besides, there is always more.

This book is intended as a course in Latin for the nibbler and the glutton alike: it may be read in considerably less than a lifetime and with infinitely less effort, and from it you may gain a good feel for the Latin language in the variety of its natural settings, past and present.

A few words about the preparation of *Latin for People*. In it we have sought to present the fundamentals of Classical Latin grammar together with some idea of the ways in which the language could actually be used as a tool for shaping reality. What else, after all, is a language for? Each of the following chapters therefore tells you something about the nuts and bolts of Latin grammar, how they may be put together and taken apart again, and to what ends. Exercises in both Latin and English are included for readers who may wish to put anything into practice, that being the only sure way of definitively getting the best of a language. The exercises of each chapter are preceded by a list of the vocabulary in order of appearance. At the end of the book appear the trots (as basic a part of the history of Latin as the first declension or Caesar's *Gallic Wars*), a general Glossary and Synopsis of the Grammar, and a few suggestions as to where to go for seconds.

LATIN FOR PEOPLE | LATINA PRO POPULO

CHAPTER I

Sling and Stone:
The Latin Language So Far

Languages are extremely elusive creatures, quite impossible to capture and very difficult to describe with any kind of precision. The main reason for this is their apparently universal tendency to change while your back is turned. Latin has been no exception. As a result, "Latin" can refer to any or all of an infinite variety of different "Latins," depending on the specific who, what, where, and when being discussed at the time—and who's doing the discussing.

This book is about a particular "Latin" which we might now try to point out in the crowd. After this has been done, more formal introductions will be in order. (They will, in fact, take up the rest of the book.) We may approach our subject from two different directions. First, we can have a look at the life and times of the Latin language and its various speakers. Having gotten a feeling for the general social contexts in which Latin has served as a medium of communication, we can then look at the inner workings of the language itself, its overall grammatical system.

Where did Latin come from and where did it go? To attempt an answer to this question, we might do best to go back to a time before there was any such thing as Latin and work forward to the present.

The story begins some 6,000 years ago just north of the Caucasus Mountains. Here seems to have lived a group of nomads, the Indo-Europeans, so called because we know for sure that they wound up in the general vicinities of India and Europe a couple of thousand years later. (They also wound up in Turkey, where they were known as the Hittites, though this fact was not discovered until the term "Indo-European" had already become firmly ensconced as the one for those people from just north of the Caucasus Mountains.)

By about 2500 B.C., some of these Indo-Europeans began to appear in Eastern Europe. They and their eastbound cousins are presumed to have spoken essentially the same language, generally called Proto-Indo-European (PIE for short). As the Indo-Europeans gradually settled down in different places, different dialects of PIE began to make their appearance, as is the rule with languages whose speakers take up residence in far-flung and relatively isolated clumps and don't stay in touch. No two communities ever develop in quite the same way, so it is hardly surprising that their linguistic habits and conventions are never quite the same, either. This is most obviously so when a group which speaks one language and has one set of customs settles in a region already inhabited by another group with a totally different language and way of looking at the cosmos, as happened with the Indo-Europeans wherever they went in those days. (Just what sorts of people were living in Europe and speaking just what sorts of languages at the time of the Indo-Europeans' arrival is unclear, but somebody was living there and they weren't, apparently, Indo-Europeans.)

Then as now, when large numbers of new neighbors move in who speak a different language from the one spoken by the natives, there is bound to be a fight about which of the two will be the one that you have to know to get a good job or at least not get left out altogether. When one wins out, as Indo-European seems to have done for the most part, the victory is never unequivocal: the people who have to learn the new language generally leave their mark on it, and this mark becomes part of the language while nobody's looking. Within a generation or two, the "official" or "high prestige" language is quite changed from the one that the fight was originally all about. So it went with Indo-European wherever the Indo-Europeans made themselves at home.

By 1000 B.C. or so, several groups of Indo-Europeans had at one time or another over the years muscled their way into Italy and settled there. Of special interest to us is one such group, the *Latīnī*, who settled in *Latium* in the western-central region of the peninsula. If this all begins to sound familiar, it will come as no surprise that by the middle of the millennium, Latium's biggest local attraction was a city called *Rōma* where the official language was *lingua Latina*.

The Latīnī did not remain settled for very long and, in consequence, their language did not long remain local. Once consolidated by the Romans—that is, by the Latīnī who lived in Rome—the

5

speakers of Latin really got down to business. First, there were the neighbors to be brought into line. These included the Etruscans to the northwest, the Ligurians (farther north and west), the Illyrians to the east and northeast, the Oscans and Umbrians to the south, the colonial Greeks (farther south), and the people living on Sicily, the *Siculī*. The first of these to be battled off were the Etruscans, a group of apparently non-Indo-European origin who held all but linguistic sway over the Latinī and many of their neighbors until 475 B.C., when the Romans, with a little help from their friends, booted them out. After a substantial but temporary setback around 390 B.C., when an invasion of Celts came over the Alps and put Rome to the sack, the Romans began their conquests in earnest, first in the north, then, more or less simultaneously, toward the west (along the southern coast of France) and toward the south (inside the Italic peninsula). By about 100 B.C. (and for nearly two hundred years thereafter), the Romans dominated all of the land touching the Mediterranean Sea, and then some.

Naturally, the Romans brought their language along wherever they went, and anybody who wanted to get a proper job with the civil service, or just stay healthy, learned it, at least after a fashion. Actually, the "their language" which the Romans took with them on their travels to new and exotic places was really two closely related but by no means identical Latins. First, there was the Latin of official business, literature, and speech-making, "high class" Latin; and there was the Latin which everybody in fact spoke, a decidedly more colloquial variety. This more colloquial variety is usually termed "Vulgar Latin," not because it was especially suited for telling dirty jokes—all languages are—but because it was spoken by the *vulgus*, that is, the people. The histories of these two Latins intertwine but are ultimately quite distinct.

What happened to Vulgar Latin is easily enough told: since this was the Latin that the advancing legions of Romans actually spoke, it was the Latin that got learned by the unlettered masses, which in those days was practically everybody. Even the people who could read and write spoke Vulgar Latin, saving the fancier spread, now generally known as Classical Latin, exclusively for writing and speechifying. (And the speechifiers who were really interested in being understood by the people used something like Vulgar Latin: St. Jerome's translation of the Bible, which appeared around A.D. 400, is not called the Vulgate for nothing.) So early on, what was learned in the cradle was the local brand of Vulgar Latin. By A.D. 600 or so, Vulgar Latin learned in the cradle was no longer really Latin, Vulgar or otherwise: in Spain, it had become an early dialect of Spanish; in France, an early dialect of French; and so on throughout the Romanized parts of Europe.

This is not to say that Vulgar Latin quietly disappeared as a unified, single language. Far from it. Vulgar Latin continued to serve as the lingua franca of the "civilized" world long after the final dismemberment of the Roman Empire, a process substantially completed by A.D. 500. The only thing was, you could no longer pick up Vulgar Latin by listening to what the folks spoke at home. You had to go out and get somebody to teach it to you out of a book. This was essentially what had happened much earlier to Classical Latin, which is the subject of this book.

As we have suggested, Classical Latin (which people wrote) and Vulgar Latin (which people spoke) were originally not all that different. Written languages generally work in the following way: first comes the spoken language. Then a system of transcribing speech is invented or, more often, borrowed from somebody else. Then it occurs to the people who know how to write that they don't have to limit their literary activities to the mere transcription of things that have actually been said. Instead, they can write down what should have been said, fix the original up a little to make it all sound better: "style" is invented and "literary language" is on its way.

Ordinarily, the literary language keeps in touch with the spoken language. In societies with a high literacy rate, the reverse also tends to hold. In such societies, the literary language tells the spoken language to pull its socks up and stand straight, and the spoken language tells the literary language not to be so damned stuffy, with the result that both stay alive and well.

However, in the time of the Roman expansion, and for quite a

7

few centuries thereafter, the literate could safely count themselves among the few rather than the many. Those who could read and write Latin during the second and first centuries before Christ therefore went about their literary business as they pleased, working out the high style of Classical Latin. In the first and second centuries of the Christian Era, when Rome was beginning to show the first signs of decay, the literate mostly toyed with a language which had been essentially fixed in the preceding two centuries. (To give an idea, the "Golden Age" of Latin literature covers the period from about 100 B.C. to A.D. 14, the end of the reign of Caesar Augustus. Then comes the "Silver Age," which peters out somewhere around A.D. 150.)

At about this time, the Roman Empire (and Classical Latin) began to fall upon hard times. Around A.D. 300, the empire split into a mostly Latin-speaking western half and a mostly Greek-speaking eastern half. For the next five to eight hundred years, the only Europeans urgently concerned with written Latin were the Christians, who were decidedly more interested in spreading the Word than they were with the high style of the Classical Age. Classical Latin at this point did not so much die as go into a state of suspended animation. It was still the kind of Latin that was taught in the Eastern Empire (which hadn't been nearly so badly hurt as the western half by the marauding Germanic tribes that terrorized Europe in the third and fourth centuries). Indeed, *the* classic Classical Latin grammar, by one Priscian, dates from A.D. 500.

With the rise of the universities in the twelfth century came a renewed interest in Latin and Latin grammar of the sort found in the grammar books, namely, "good" or "Classical" Latin. The standard academic program of the day, the *trivium* and *quadrivium* (grammar, logic, rhetoric and music, arithmetic, geometry, and astronomy), prominently featured the study of Classical Latin grammar. When the Renaissance arrived a couple of centuries later, it brought with it a rekindled enthusiasm for the "classics" of both Greek and Latin, as well as for the languages in which these had been written.

8

From the Renaissance, it is a short jump to the present day when, if nobody writes learned treatises in Latin so that everybody in the scholarly community may be able to read them (as was the custom until this century), Latin is still very much with us, continuing to exert a profound influence on our own language, as on others.

This influence is of two orders. First, Latin has provided (and continues to provide) an incredible proportion of our minimum daily requirement of vocabulary. Even though English, like German, Danish, and Swedish, is descended from the Germanic branch of the Indo-European family, its vocabulary is preponderantly Latinate. And second, by providing us with words, Latin has also provided us with the concepts which those words express. What else, after all, are words for if not to *mean* something? As a result, the Latin language has continued to play a substantial role in shaping the way we look at the world, since we can't help but filter the world through our language. To know something about Latin, then, is to know something about how and why we perceive the cosmos as we do.

Latin, like all other languages, has a grammatical system. Indeed, it is largely thanks to the early grammarians of Classical Latin that we have the framework in which to discuss grammar that we do. (If the Latin grammarians borrowed freely from the Greeks the bulk of their terms and their notions, it was all of a piece with the way the Romans operated in those days.)

Broadly speaking, a language's "grammatical system" is a set of linguistic units (of various shapes and sizes) plus a set of rules that tell you how they may be combined: "meanings" go together in certain ways to form "ideas"; "words," to make "sentences"; "sounds," to make "words"; and so on. For now, it will be convenient to divide Latin's grammatical system into two parts, its "sound system" and its "grammatical system proper." We will have a look at the grammatical system proper first.

As good an introduction as any to Latin's grammatical system proper is provided by the old-timers, like Varro (first century B.C.), Donatus (fourth century A.D.), and Priscian (late fifth century A.D.). For them, the main order of business was to establish a workable system for classifying Latin words. This involved looking at the vocabulary of literary Latin and asking the following questions:

(1) What kinds of semantic properties can words share?
(2) What kinds of syntactic properties can they share?
(3) What purely formal properties can they share?
(4) How would the Greeks have handled everything?

With the possible exception of the last, these questions were eminently logical. Linguists are still asking them, in fact. Even the last question was not as unreasonable as it might appear. For one thing, Greek and Latin have a great deal in common (not altogether surprisingly, considering their shared Indo-European origin). Perhaps more important was the simple fact that the Greeks had been thinking about the first three questions themselves in the study of their own language and had already come up with some useful ways of classifying words. Why go to the bother of inventing something when you might be able to borrow it from the Greeks?

The upshot was a general agreement on the following categories: *nōmen, prōnōmen, verbum, adverbium, participium, praepositiō, conjunctiō*, and *interjectiō*. Of these, all but the last were lifted in virtually mint condition from the Greeks; and English, one of the most notorious borrowers of all time, has followed suit by lifting them all. A quick look at the kinds of words that belonged to each of these categories may be helpful.

Nōmen originally meant "name." A word was said to be a *nōmen* if it "named" a substance or quality. Thus, "Caesar," "Rome," "cat," "stone," "truth," "marvelous," and "green" would all have belonged to the class *nōmen*. Some of the members of the *nōmen* family could be used to describe or "modify" others. (A grammarian would have said that the quality named by a word could

10

be attributed to the quality or substance named by another, but that's a grammarian for you.) A *nōmen* that was used to describe another was called a *nōmen adjectīvum*, which means, roughly, "an assistant noun." Thus, in the sentences "Say, here's a marvelous green" and "Say, here's a marvelous green stone," "marvelous," "green," and "stone" would each have been considered a *nōmen*. "Marvelous" would have been a *nōmen adjectīvum* in both sentences; "green" would have been a regular *nōmen* in the first sentence and a *nōmen adjectīvum* in the second; and "stone" would have been a regular *nōmen*. In English, we would classify "marvelous" and "green" as adjectives, of course, and "stone" as a noun. We would say that "green" was used "substantively" in the first sentence, which is simply a way of avoiding calling a *nōmen* a noun.

So one reason why the early grammarians classed nouns and adjectives together was to avoid the question of what to call an adjective that is used as a noun (and what to call a noun that is used as an adjective, as in "Say, that's a marvelous car radio," where "car" looks for all the world like an adjective): if they're all the same part of speech, what's the problem?

Besides, there were other properties shared by nouns and adjectives in Latin. For one thing, all the members of the *nōmen* class had the same structure. Each could be seen as a sequence of two elements: a stem followed by an ending. The stem carried the meaning of the word, essentially, while the ending told you whether the word was singular or plural and gave you some idea of what it was doing in the sentence. (English still bears the faint trace of this Indo-European delicacy in such noun sets as "cat, cat's, cats, cats'" and "dog, dog's, dogs, dogs'," where "cat-" and "dog-" are stems and the rest are endings.) Depending on how you reckon it, there were six or twelve different kinds of ending that all members of the *nōmen* class carried around with them. These different kinds of ending are called cases, and they are: nominative (singular), vocative (singular), genitive (singular), dative (singular), accusative (singular), ablative (singular), nominative (plural), vocative (plural), genitive (plural), dative (plural), accusative (plural), and ablative (plural).

11

Nouns—we will look at adjectives presently—appeared in the nominative case, that is, with a nominative ending, chiefly when they were the subject of a verb. (In the sentence "George ate his shoes," "George" would appear in the nominative case.) The vocative case was used for directly addressing somebody or something. (In the sentence "George, you're fired," "George" would appear in the vocative case.) The genitive case was mostly used to express possession. (In the sentence "George's parents were not surprised," "George" would be in the genitive case.) A noun appears in the dative case when it is an indirect object. (In the sentences "I gave George an improving book" and "I baked George a cake," "George" would appear in the dative case.) Direct objects get to be in the accusative case: "I give you George" (in the accusative). The ablative, sometimes known as the Latin case (because Greek didn't have one) or the sixth case (because Greek had the other five) has a number of uses. (How the Greeks managed to get along without an ablative case is a mystery.) In the following sentences, "George" would be in the ablative: "This book was written by George," "I went to school with George," "With George at the helm (as long as George is at the helm), we have nothing to fear."

Two more things must be said about nouns and endings. First, each noun in Latin belonged to one of three categories, or genders. (The word "gender" comes from the Latin *genus*, which means "family, race, sort, variety.") These are masculine, feminine, and neuter. (*Neuter* simply means "neither" in Latin.) For all practical purposes, they might as well have been vanilla, chocolate, and strawberry, since sex has very little to do with grammatical gender— *all* nouns are one gender or another, most are either masculine or feminine, and, when you think of it, an awful lot of nouns are simply asexual. The one thing going for the traditional classification is that, by and large, nouns designating female people or animals are feminine in gender; those designating masculine people or animals, masculine. For the rest, it is hit or miss.

So when you learn a new Latin noun, you have to ask whether it's masculine, feminine, or neuter. You also have to ask which "declension" it belongs to. A declension, of which there are basically

12

five in Latin, is a specific set of case endings. The best of all possible worlds in which there had to be both gender and declension would naturally work it so that for each gender there would be one set of endings and one set only. Apparently, the Indo-Europeans had other things on their minds than the best of all possible worlds when they invented their language. In Latin, the fit between gender and declension is consequently rather sloppy, though not entirely random: two of the five declensions hardly get used at all; one that does get used is almost exclusively for feminine gender, another is almost exclusively for masculine and neuter, and the third is catch as catch can.

Adjectives are easy once you have gotten past the nouns. Adjectives have to "agree" with the nouns they modify in number, gender, and case. That is, singular adjectives go with singular nouns; plural, with plural; masculine, with masculine; nominative, with nominative; and so on. Because adjectives belong to the same declensions as nouns, once you have learned the endings for nouns, you are home free, at least as far as the *nōmen* family is concerned.

As for the other parts of speech mentioned earlier, they are not nearly as far out as the *nōmen* (which, after all, is not as far out as all *that*). The *prōnōmen* class contains a mercifully small number of words that fill in for their *nōmen* cousins. For example, instead of having to say "One morning Caesar looked into *Caesar's* mirror and said to *Caesar*, '*Caesar* knows, *Caesar* should knock over Gaul,' " one can say, "One morning, Caesar looked into *his* mirror and said to *himself*, '*You* know, *you* should knock over Gaul.' " The members of the *prōnōmen* class (otherwise known as pronouns) also come with the standard issue of cases.

Verbum originally meant "word." Later, of course, it came to mean a particular kind of word, the kind that tells you what the action is: a verb. Latin verbs, like Latin nouns, adjectives, and pronouns, can be seen as sequences of stems and endings. Again, the stem carries the basic meaning of the word and the endings handle the details. The endings of the verb tell you who the subject is, that is, who is doing the action expressed by the verb.

There are six possibilities, each with a different personal ending first person singular (I, myself), second person singular (you, your-self), third person singular (he, himself; she, herself; it, itself; George; Mary; the cat), first person plural (we, ourselves), second person plural (you, yourselves), and third person plural (they, themselves). English again shows only a trace of the original Indo-European system of stems and endings in "I cry," "he cries," "I cried," to which may be added "thou criest" which, of course, nobody actually *says* anymore. The endings of the verb also tell you when the action is happening (or happened), that is, what "tense" the verb is in. ("Tense" comes, ultimately, from Latin *tempus*, which means "time.")

Two further pieces of information are carried by the verb endings. The first of these is whether the verb is active or passive, that is, whether the subject of the verb is doing the action or the action is being done to him (or her or it). Latin would have one verb form for "(I) was fleeced" and another for "(I) fleeced (somebody)." The final piece of information carried by the verb ending is what "mood" the verb is, indicative, or subjunctive. Mood takes a bit of explaining. Forget about it for the time being. What is important for now is that there are four things that verb endings have to tell you, and the price of this wealth of information is that you have a lot of endings to learn. Well, not *that* many, really, and a pleasant side benefit is: languages like Latin that are big on endings are often quite relaxed about word order—you can put most of the con-stituents of a Latin sentence pretty much where you please and still be perfectly understood.

The *adverbium* is—*mīrābile dictū* – the adverb, the word that tells you *how* the action is performed—quickly, slowly, foolishly, and so on. No problem here.

The *participium*, or participle, in Latin is a cross between a *verbum* and a *nōmen*: it has case endings like a *nōmen*, but it has a distinctly verbal aspect. Case endings aside, the Latin participles, of which there are four varieties, are not very different from the English ones. (Consider, for example, the sentence "When the going gets tough, the tough get going," which, in addition to its aphoristic

14

merit, has fifty percent of all you will ever have to know about participles. The first "going" is a gerund, that is, a verb form functioning as a noun; and the second "going" is a real verb form. Both "goings" are participles in English and Latin.)

That leaves the *praepositiō*, or preposition; the *conjunctiō*, or conjunction; and the *interjectiō*, or interjection. Prepositions are small endingless words that come right before a *nōmen* (or *prōnōmen*) and tell you "where," "how," "when," and sometimes "why," as in: "*under* water," "*with* a smile," "*before* the Ides of March," and "*for* no particular reason." Conjunctions are small endingless words that come between two (or more) of the same parts of speech and join them together, as in "George *and* Mary," "they laughed *or* cried." Interjections, like "hey," "fooey," and "damn!" are none of the above.

If the early grammarians get high marks for their handling of the grammatical system proper, they may perhaps be forgiven their less than exemplary treatment of Latin's "sound system." Even today, there are those who hold that if you take care of the sense, the sounds will take care of themselves, a methodological principle which is great for saving paper but which is apt to result in certain difficulties for later learners of the language.

The variety of sounds which people produce in conversing in their language is infinite. No two sounds are ever quite identical. Fortunately, they don't have to be, because the speakers of a language have a tacit agreement that all speech sounds falling within a particular range will be considered to be the same sound, and all those falling outside that range, different. The number of contrasting ranges that a language uses in this way is generally quite small. (Most languages make do comfortably with twenty or thirty.) The way you discover where the boundaries are between ranges in a language is to play some variation on the old Same/Different or Minimal Pair game with a card-carrying native speaker of the language: "Did you say 'Hi' or did you say 'How' (or 'He' or 'Who') and are these the same thing or what?" (Note that it will not do to play this game with a native speaker of some other language, for it is rare indeed that two different languages wind up having the exact same inventory of sound ranges.)

What were the sound ranges of Latin, and how can anyone be sure, since there are no native speakers to play the Minimal Pair game with anymore? The Romans and their heirs have provided a number of clues. For one thing, somebody told them about the alphabet fairly early in the game. This ingenious Near Eastern invention had worked its way onto the Italic peninsula in a variety of forms by the fourth century B.C. (For a time, there were three major contenders for the title of official alphabet on the peninsula, the so-called Illyrian, Italic, and Etruscan scripts, the last of which eventually won out. The Etruscans themselves should have done so well.)

We also have something like firsthand testimony from the early Latin grammarians, people whose native language was Latin. To be sure, the early grammarians were letter- rather than sound-oriented and their rules for pronouncing the letters of the alphabet were less systematic than we'd like. Moreover, there is ample reason to suspect that the Latin which they wrote about and the Latin which they in fact spoke were never quite the same. But later grammarians weren't all that more thorough on the phonetic end of things, and they were certainly lax when it came to checking with native speakers of the language.

In a way, the best information about Latin's sounds is provided by the modern-day Romance languages, Portuguese, Spanish, Catalan, Provençal, French, Rhaeto-Romance, Rumanian, Italian, and their many dialects. This "best" information merely has to be finessed a little.

Suppose that when we compare the vocabularies of these languages we find many striking similarities, such as the following:

Spanish	puerta	puentes	puerco
French	porte	ponts	porc
Italian	porta	ponti	porco
	door	bridges	swine

It's a safe bet that Spanish, French, and Italian didn't just happen to make up nearly identical words for "door" (and "bridges" and "swine" and many, many more). Nor should it come as any great surprise that the Latin words for "door," "bridges," and "swine" are *porta, pontēs*, and *porcus*. Even if we'd never heard of Latin, we would still presumably have reasoned that these languages are so similar, not only in their vocabularies and sound systems, but in their grammatical systems proper, that they must share a common ancestor. That is, they must have evolved from the same language or from different dialects of the same language.

In any case, whether we *know* that the Romance languages have a common origin or we have merely *inferred* as much, it all boils down to the same thing. When we observe some feature, like the unaspirated "p" sound in the words just cited, which is shared by the Romance languages and is probably not the result of borrowing or "independent innovation," we assume that that feature was part of the parent language or was shared by the parental dialects of that language. By this method of comparing the sound systems of the Romance languages, seeing what characteristics they share in common, we eventually arrive at a set of sound ranges, which we hypothesize were shared by the dialects of Latin where it all began. The availability of Latin grammars and numerous Latin texts guard against any howling blunders and help to fill in the missing pieces. It doesn't hurt a bit that we also have Old French, Old Spanish, Vulgar Latin, and other texts of intermediate ages between Classical Latin and the modern Romance languages.

Latin's sound system almost without a doubt contained the following:

p		t	k		
b		d	g		
	f	s			h
m		n	ŋ		
		l			
		r			
w			y		

The p, t, and k sounds were probably unaspirated, that is, when you made a Latin p, t, or k sound, it entered the world unaccompanied by the little puff of air that attends the birth of all such sounds in English (except when they follow an s, as in "spot," "start," and "skip," or are swallowed at the end of a word, as in "stop," "start," and "stick"). The t, d, n, l, and r were probably made with the tip of the tongue against the upper teeth; the s, with the tip of the tongue against the lower teeth. The Ɖ is essentially the nasal sound which we have in English in "si*ng*," "ri*ng*er," and the like. The r was doubtless of the flap, or trill, variety found in Spanish, Italian, or highly theatrical English.

These were represented by the following letters of the alphabet:

p		t	c and q	
b		d	g	
	f	s		h
m		n	n (before c, q, g)	
		l		
		r		
v (u)			j (i)	

A final note on the consonants before moving on to vowels: the evidence from the Romance languages strongly suggests that Latin made a phonetic distinction between single and double "twin" consonant sounds, much as modern Italian does in such words as *fato* (fate) and *fatto* (deed). In Italian, this distinction involves a longer vowel and a more quickly released consonant *versus* a shorter vowel and a not-so-quickly released consonant.

Latin also had, as far as we can tell, ten vowels, five short and five long. The short vowels probably differed from their long counterparts in two respects. First, the long vowels were held longer. Second, there was probably a difference in timbre, a difference in the position of your tongue when making one vowel as opposed to another, similar to that found in modern German.

Latin's long vowels were *comparable* to the vowels in English "meet," "mate," "Ma," "moot," and "mote." The "short" vowels were comparable to those in English "mit," "met," "Ma" (only more perfunctory), "foot," and "motley" (if you're from Bawston, Massachusetts). They were represented as follows:

ī	(m<u>ee</u>t)	i	(m<u>i</u>t)
ē	(m<u>a</u>te)	e	(m<u>e</u>t)
ā	(M<u>aaa</u>)	a	(M<u>a</u>)
ū	(m<u>oo</u>t)	u	(f<u>oo</u>t)
ō	(m<u>o</u>te)	o	(m<u>o</u>tley)

Latin had three diphthongs as well: "ay" (as in English "buy"), which was spelled *ae*; "oy" (as in English "boy"), which was spelled *oe*; and "ow" (as in English "wow"), which was spelled *au*.

Finally, Latin had an admirably straightforward set of rules for stressing words on the right syllable. The rules are as follows. (1) If the vowel in the next-to-last syllable of a word is long, stress it and ask no questions. (2) If the vowel in the next-to-last syllable is short, either of two things can happen. If the vowel is followed by two or more consonants, it is considered long by position and it gets stressed. Otherwise, stress the vowel in the next-to-next-to-last (antepenultimate) syllable and call it a day.

CHAPTER II

Nouns to Nouns

The inhabitants of Magna Graecia (Greater Greece) were among the very last on the Italic peninsula to be "Romanized." They had long formed the Greek-speaking sole of what was to become an officially Latin-speaking boot. Of the many interesting and influential people who lived there at one time or another, perhaps the most remarkable was an immigrant from Samos at the end of the sixth century B.C., Pythagoras.

Pythagoras and his followers were first and foremost a religious sect, very big on cosmic symmetry and pattern. Not surprisingly, they were very heavily into mathematics, their researches revealing all sorts of hitherto unsuspected symmetries and patterns there for the taking. Small wonder that they were fond of the sphere and the circle, finding one or the other at every turn. The earth was a sphere, the other celestial spheres moved in circular orbit, and the case forms of a *nōmen* (noun or adjective) were radii in the upper right-hand quadrant of a circle.

The nominative case was considered to be the vertical radius; the others, oblique radii, that is, neither vertical nor horizontal. The nominative was therefore known as the "upright" case (*cāsus rēctus*) and the others, as the "oblique" cases (*cāsūs oblīquī*).

The term case (*cāsus*) comes from the verb "to fall," the idea being that when you ran through the complete set of case forms of a *nōmen*, you started from straight up and down in the nominative and fell precipitously through the vocative, genitive, dative, accusative, and (in Latin) ablative, coming to a crashing halt at fourteen past the hour, and not a moment too soon. This makes the upright case a contradiction in terms, of course, but what right-thinking Pythagorean, having come this far, is going to quibble?

The process of running—or falling—through the complete set of case forms for a *nōmen* was called "declining": to decline is to turn away from, in this instance, to turn away from the nominative and make a break for it along the perimeter. To turn down, we might say. In any event, if Latin has five declensions, this means that there are five possible tracks around the nominal circle. We will have a look at two of them here.

The first declension is probably so named because it is the most straightforward and, therefore, the one you get to hear about first in a Latin grammar. Samples of first declension nouns are:

SINGULAR

	FEM	FEM
NOM	matella	īnsula
VOC	matella	īnsula
GEN	matellae	īnsulae
DAT	matellae	īnsulae
ACC	matellam	īnsulam
ABL	matellā	īnsulā

NOM	matellae	īnsulae
VOC	matellae	īnsulae
GEN	matellārum	īnsulārum
DAT	matellīs	īnsulīs
ACC	matellās	īnsulās
ABL	matellīs	īnsulīs

Matella, matellae chamber pot; *insula, īnsulae* island.

Matell- and *īnsul-* are stems; *-a, -a, -ae, -am, -ā, -ae, -ae, -ārum, -īs, -ās,* and *-īs,* the set of endings of the first declension. Since a number of these are identical in appearance, the question immediately arises: when someone says *matellae,* for example, how do you know which case form it is, as it could equally well be genitive singular (of a chamber pot), dative singular (to a chamber pot), nominative plural (chamber pots), or vocative plural (O chamber pots!)? The answer is to have a look at the rest of what that someone is saying and see which reading makes the most—or any—sense.

Some examples:

Īnsula nōn in Galliā (est). (The) island is not in Gaul.
  Īnsula is in the nominative singular because it's the subject; *Galliā* is in the ablative singular because it's the object of the preposition *in*; and *est* is in parentheses because literate speakers of Latin would probably not have bothered to put it in a sentence like this, but would have left it understood.
Agricolae matellae in Galliā (sunt). The farmer's chamber pots are in Gaul. (The alternate reading "The chamber pots' farmers are in Gaul," while thinkable, is less likely.) *Agricolae* is the genitive singular of *agricola* (farmer), and *matellae* is the nominative plural of *matella.*
Puella matellam agricolae dat. The girl gives the chamber pot to the farmer. *Puella* is nominative singular, being the subject; *matellam* is accusative singular because that's the case that direct objects

22

get to be in in Latin; and *agricolae* is in the dative because the
farmer is being given something. (Dative comes from the verb
"to give," of which *dat* is a form.)

The so-called second declension is a little more complicated than
the first, but not much. We mentioned earlier that Latin nouns are
either masculine, feminine, or neuter in grammatical gender. Most
of the nouns of the first declension happen to be feminine in gender,
the tiny number of exceptions, such as *agricola* (farmer) and *nauta*
(sailor), being words that designate male people. All nouns of the
first declension, regardless of gender, are declined in the manner just
shown. The second declension is made up of both masculine and
neuter nouns and these are declined slightly differently from each
other:

SINGULAR

	MASC	NEUT
NOM	mundus	bellum
VOC	munde	bellum
GEN	mundī	bellī
DAT	mundō	bellō
ACC	mundum	bellum
ABL	mundō	bellō

PLURAL

NOM	mundī	bella
VOC	mundī	bella
GEN	mundōrum	bellōrum
DAT	mundīs	bellīs
ACC	mundōs	bella
ABL	mundīs	bellīs

Mundus, mundī world; *bellum, bellī* war.

23

Mund- and *bell-* are stems, and the only appreciable difference between masculine and neuter nouns of this declension is to be found in the nominative, vocative, and accusative case endings. It is a general feature of neuter nouns that they have the same ending for the nominative, vocative, and accusative, making less work for the student of Latin, which is all to the good.

Neuters are not unique in having the same ending for the nominative and vocative. *Most* Latin nouns and adjectives make no such distinction. In fact, the only ones which *do* have separate case endings for the nominative and vocative are those of the second declension, like *mundus*, which end in *-us* in the nominative singular and *-e* in the vocative singular. And not all such *-us* forms obey this rule: those ending in *-ius* in the nominative singular, like *fīlius* (son), don't have a different vocative form. "O son" is *O fīlius,* and that's that. So, for all practical purposes, the only time you have to go to the bother of learning a vocative ending is for masculine nouns and adjectives of the second declension which end in *-us* but not *-ius*.

This is not quite all there is to the second declension, however, as witness the following:

SINGULAR

NOM	adulter	ager
VOC	adulter	ager
GEN	adulterī	agrī
DAT	adulterō	agrō
ACC	adulterum	agrum
ABL	adulterō	agrō

PLURAL

NOM	adulterī	agrī
VOC	adulterī	agrī
GEN	adulterōrum	agrōrum
DAT	adulterīs	agrīs
ACC	adulterōs	agrōs
ABL	adulterīs	agrīs

Adulter, adulterī adulterer; *ager, agrī* field.

Nouns of the *adulter* type might be said to differ from those like *mundus* in not having any visible (or audible) ending in the nominative and vocative singular. Nouns like *ager* don't seem to have any ending in the nominative and vocative singular, and there is a further wrinkle: the *e* of the stem seems to disappear when we arrive at the genitive singular and is never heard of again. How you know whether to decline a noun that ends in *-er* in the nominative like *adulter* or like *ager* is simple: you look it up in the dictionary where the nominative will be followed by the genitive singular form, which tells all. Thus, *socer, socerī* (father-in-law) versus *cancer, cancrī* (crab). Fortunately, most second-declension nouns are like *mundus, mundī* and *bellum, bellī*.

Adjectives of the first and second declensions are perfectly straightforward once you've encountered their nominal cousins. Mostly, they are like *triquetrus, triquetra, triquetrum* (three-cornered).

SINGULAR

	MASC	FEM	NEUT
NOM	triquetrus	triquetra	triquetrum
VOC	triquetre	triquetra	triquetrum
GEN	triquetrī	triquetrae	triquetrī
DAT	triquetrō	triquetrae	triquetrō
ACC	triquetrum	triquetram	triquetrum
ABL	triquetrō	triquetrā	triquetrō

PLURAL

	MASC	FEM	NEUT
NOM	triquetrī	triquetrae	triquetra
VOC	triquetrī	triquetrae	triquetra
GEN	triquetrōrum	triquetrārum	triquetrōrum
DAT	triquetrīs	triquetrīs	triquetrīs
ACC	triquetrōs	triquetrās	triquetra
ABL	triquetrīs	triquetrīs	triquetrīs

The ones that aren't like these — and most are — are either like *līber, lībera, līberum* (free) or else like *taeter, taetra, taetrum* (foul, abominable).

NOM	līber	lībera	līberum
VOC	līber	lībera	līberum
GEN	līberī	līberae	līberī
	etc.	etc.	etc.

PLURAL

NOM	līberī	līberae	lībera
VOC	līberī	līberae	lībera
GEN	līberōrum	līberārum	līberōrum
	etc.	etc.	etc.

SINGULAR

NOM	taeter	taetra	taetrum
VOC	taeter	taetra	taetrum
GEN	taetrī	taetrae	taetrī
	etc.	etc.	etc.

PLURAL

NOM	taetrī	taetrae	taetra
VOC	taetrī	taetrae	taetra
GEN	taetrōrum	taetrārum	taetrōrum
	etc.	etc.	etc.

A hint and two reminders about adjectives, then some vocabulary. First, the hint: when you have a noun that could be declined one way or another, the dictionary puts you onto the right one by giving the nominative singular and genitive singular forms; for adjectives, the dictionary simply gives the masculine, feminine, and neuter forms of the nominative singular from which you can deduce all you need to know. Usually. (When there is anything exceptional in the declension, they generally tell you in the dictionary as a point of interest.)

The two reminders: adjectives "agree" with the nouns they modify in both number and gender and case, which means that if you want to modify, say, a masculine singular noun appearing in the ablative, then you need an adjective of similar persuasion, as, *in agrō triquetrō* (in a three-cornered field). Again, adjectives can be used substantively, as though they were nouns: *bonī, malī, et taetrī* (the good, the bad, and the abominable [people]) or *bona, mala, et taetra* (the good, the bad, and the abominable [things]).

Vocabulary

The vocabulary is given as it would be in the dictionary, listing the nominative and genitive singular forms for nouns and the mascu-line, feminine, and neuter nominative singular for adjectives. Words are given in their order of appearance in this chapter; they appear alphabetically in the Glossary at the end of the book.

matella, matellae (f.) chamber pot

īnsula, īnsulae (f.) island

nōn not, no

in in, on (with the ablative). Latin has another *in* which means "into, against" with the accusative.

Gallia, Galliae (f.) Gaul

est is

agricola, agricolae (m.) farmer

sunt (they) are

puella, puellae (f.) girl

dat gives

nauta, nautae (m.) sailor

mundus, mundī (m.) world

bellum, bellī (n.) war

fīlius, fīliī (m.) son

adulter, adulterī (m.) adulterer

ager, agrī (m.) field

socer, socerī (m.) father-in-law

cancer, cancrī (m.) crab

triquetrus, triquetra, triquetrum three-cornered

līber, lībera, līberum free. In the plural, *līberī* is the customary word for "children." In the singular and with a capital L, *Līber* is Bacchus. Finally, *līber* is not to be confused with *liber, librī* (m.) book.

taeter, taetra, taetrum foul,
abominable, noisome
bonus, bona, bonum good
malus, mala, malum bad. Not
to be confused with *mālum,
mālī* (n.) apple.
et and
sed but
locus, locī (m.) place, location
idōneus, idōnea, idōneum fit
for, suitable for. When A is
suitable for B, *idōneus*
agrees with A in number,
gender, and case, and B
appears in the dative. Thus,
in locō idōneō matellīs in a
place suitable for chamber
pots.
fīlia, fīliae (f.) daughter
super on, above (with the
accusative)
sub under (with the ablative)
Britannia, Britanniae (f.)
Britain

I. Translate into English

a. *Bellum in Galliā malum, sed in matellā taetrum.*
b. *Līberī līberī adulterī.*
c. *Mundus locus idōneus īnsulīs.*
d. *Nauta agricolae cancrum dat; agricola, mālum nautae.*
e. *Agricolae fīlia bona agrōrum dat socerō.*
f. *Fīlius nautae super īnsulam; īnsula, sub matellā.*
g. *Mundus adulterī triquetrus.*
h. *Britannia īnsula nōn idōnea bellō.*

II. Translate into Latin

a. An island is not a suitable place for an adulterer.
b. The fields are under the farmers and the world is under the
fields.
c. A father-in-law does not give good things to an adulterer.

d. Books are good; but children, noisome.
e. In England, an adulterer gives the girls good books; but in Gaul, crabs.
f. O sons and daughters of Gaul, the apples of England are foul!
g. The sailor's son is in a place suitable for sailors' sons.
h. Gaul is not a three-cornered island.

CHAPTER III

Evens and Ends

When the Pythagoreans decided that it would be handy to distinguish between those numbers which could be divided by two and those which couldn't, they termed the evens "perfect" numbers; and the odds, "uncommon, extraordinary." The Latins spoke of equal (*pār*) and unequal (*impār*) numbers, and we speak of even and odd, the implication always being that if it can be divided by two, it's great, and if it can't, there's something wrong with it.

The original Indo-Europeans were so fond of the number 2 that they set up a special grammatical category called the dual, which contrasted with both the singular and the plural. Nouns and adjectives could be singular, dual, or plural, as could forms of the verb, and there were different endings for each. If you wanted to talk about something singular, like George or the cat, then you used the appropriate singular forms; and if you wanted to talk about three or more, then you used the plural. But if it was a question of George's two feet or some other boxed set of two, you used the dual. Thus, if all scholars of Latin are liars except for the two authors of this book (and I'm not so sure about one of them), "all," "scholars," "are," and "liars" would be plural forms, "the," "two," "authors," and "them" would be in the dual, and "Latin," "this," "book," "I," " 'm," and "one" would be singular.

Most of the Indo-European languages eventually merged the dual with the plural. Latin has reluctantly given up all but the memory of the dual and two reminders: the words for "two" (*duo*) and "both" (*ambō*) which are declined as follows:

	MASC		FEM		NEUT	
NOM	duo	ambō	duae	ambae	duo	ambō
VOC	duo	ambō	duae	ambae	duo	ambō
GEN	duōrum	ambōrum	duārum	ambārum	duōrum	ambōrum
DAT	duōbus	ambōbus	duābus	ambābus	duōbus	ambōbus
ACC	duōs	ambōs	duās	ambās	duo	ambō
ABL	duōbus	ambōbus	duābus	ambābus	duōbus	ambōbus

Duo, duae, duo and *ambō, ambae, ambō* are treated as though they were regular, everyday plural adjectives in Latin. That is, what they modify are plural nouns: *duo mundī* (two worlds), *in ambōbus locīs* (in both places), *duae agricolae fīliae* (two farmer's daughters), *super ambās matellās triquetrās* (on both three-cornered chamber pots), *locus idōneus ambōbus bellīs* (a place suitable for both wars).

Latin has another word for "two" that is worthy of mention here: *bīnī, bīnae, bīna*, which is declined like *bonī, bonae, bona*, the plural of *bonus, bona, bonum. Bīnī, bīnae, bīna* means "two (of the same sort), a pair." Thus, the *agricola glōriōsus* (braggart farmer) might say, *"Bīnōs agrōs habeō, pirōs in dexterō et mālōs in sinistrō"* ("I have a pair of fields, pear trees in the right-hand one and apple trees in the left-hand one"). One more modest might simply remark, *"Duōs agrōs habeō, pōmōs in ambōbus"* ("I have a couple of fields, fruit trees in both"), and let it go at that.

The Indo-European distinction "one, two, many" apparently proved to be one too many for the Latini, and the dual was quietly put out to pasture and was never heard of again. Actually, when you think of it, what this amounted to was giving up a three-way number distinction in favor of a split down the middle: they had to kill the dual to save it. The Latins were generally pretty good at turning three into two. Witness the way they handled their three-way gender distinction: masculine, feminine, and neither of the two (*neuter, neutra, neutrum* neither). They even went to the trouble to coin the term *tertium quid* (literally, third whatsis) to designate, in Mr. Webster's words, "something that escapes a division into two groups that are supposed to be exhaustive," like, neither dead nor alive. (The Theory of Logical Types, unfortunately, has come too late to be of any help to the Romans.)

This is not to say that speakers of Latin found the number three totally inimical. Latin's verb system features the number three quite prominently, there being three "persons" (each with a singular and a plural designation) who can be subjects of verbs. These are the so-called first person (singular "I" and plural "we"), the second person (singular "you" and plural "you [yourselves] "), and the third person (singular "he, she, it, George, the cat" and plural "they, the cats," etc.).

Traditionally, there are said to be four conjugation classes, that is, four slightly different sets of endings that go on the ends of verb stems. (Conjugation literally means yoking together.) Actually, there are five such classes, as will become clear from the following examples of the present (active indicative):

32

SING	1.	vastō	arō	habeō	videō
	2.	vastās	arās	habēs	vidēs
	3.	vastat	arat	habet	videt
PLUR	1.	vastāmus	arāmus	habēmus	vidēmus
	2.	vastātis	arātis	habētis	vidētis
	3.	vastant	arant	habent	vident

Vastō I lay waste, I'm laying waste; *arō* I plow, I'm plowing; *habeō*
I have, I'm having; *videō* I see, I'm seeing. Note that where English
has two present active indicative tenses, "I X" and "I'm Xing,"
Latin has but one that we translate sometimes one way, sometimes
the other, depending on which English version sounds better.

SING	1.	currō	agō	faciō	capiō
	2.	curris	agis	facis	capis
	3.	currit	agit	facit	capit
PLUR	1.	currimus	agimus	facimus	capimus
	2.	curritis	agitis	facitis	capitis
	3.	currunt	agunt	faciunt	capiunt

Currō I run, I'm running; *agō* I lead, I'm leading; *faciō* I do, I make,
I'm doing, I'm making; *capiō* I seize, I'm seizing.

SING	1.	veniō	audiō
	2.	venīs	audīs
	3.	venit	audit
PLUR	1.	venīmus	audīmus
	2.	venītis	audītis
	3.	veniunt	audiunt

Veniō I come, I'm coming; *audiō* I hear, I'm hearing.

Where these differ from each other from class to class is not so
much in the endings but, rather, in what comes just before the

endings. In the first conjugation, exemplified here by *vastō* and *arō*, what comes just before the endings is an *a* (sometimes long and sometimes short, and it's a good idea to learn where they come, as this distribution of longs and shorts runs through a good deal of the Latin verb system). This vowel is called a theme vowel and it will appear in virtually all of the other tenses of the verb. The second conjugation, exemplified by *habeō* and *videō*, differs hardly at all from the first: where *vastō* and *arō* have an *a*, *habeō* and *videō* have an *e*. The second conjugation even goes so far as to stick this *e* into the first person singular form for good measure. *Currō*, *agō*, *faciō*, and *capiō* are all traditionally classed in the third conjugation, even though *faciō* and *capiō* seem to have snuck in an *i* in the first person singular and third person plural forms. Otherwise, the third conjugation differs from the first and second in having an *i* instead of an *a* or *e*, which have already been spoken for. (A further difference is that the third conjugation doesn't have these long vowels in the present the way the others do.) Finally, if you are still counting, the fourth conjugation, to which *veniō* and *audiō* belong, tenaciously maintains its thematic *i* vowel throughout, making it "long" where *vastō*, *arō* and *habeō*, *videō* have long vowels, and making it short elsewhere.

As you have probably already guessed, the way you know which conjugation class has which verbs in it is to look up the verbs in the dictionary. Traditionally, again, Latin verbs are listed under the first person singular active indicative form, just as nouns and adjectives are listed under the nominative singular. As the dictionary supplies you with the genitive of nouns to tell all, so it gives you the principal parts of the verb—namely, the first person singular present active indicative; the infinitive; and a couple of other forms which we need not worry about here, the first person singular perfect active indicative, and the past participle.

All you really need to know to be able to conjugate a verb in the present active indicative in Latin is the first person singular and the infinitive: *vastō*, *vastāre* is easy because the infinitive has *ā*; *habeō*, *habēre* is even easier, since verbs of the second conjugation are the only ones that have that *e* in the first person singular and are also the only ones with *ē* in the infinitive; *veniō, venīre* has to be fourth conjugation because that's the only class with *ī* in the infinitive; *currō, currere* can't be any of the above because of the short vowel in the infinitive, and it can't be like *faciō, facere* because it doesn't have the *i* in the first person singular.

Well, perhaps that's not all you really need to know, as there is the matter of the endings and which vowels go where, but that's not so much. Besides, because each "person" (singular and plural) gets a different verb ending, you don't have to worry about learning any pronouns for a while—the subject of *vastō* can only be "I"; the subject of *vastās*, "you (yourself)," and so on. The Latini were casual about pronouns themselves, simply omitting the subject and letting the verb do all the work as often as not.

A final gloss on the number 2: here are the forms of the present active indicative of two very useful and wildly irregular Latin verbs, the verb "to be" and the verb "to be able":

SING	1.	sum	possum
	2.	es	potes
	3.	est	potest
PLUR	1.	sumus	possumus
	2.	estis	potestis
	3.	sunt	possunt

Esse to be; *posse* to be able. *Possum* is easy enough once *sum* has been mastered: just take the forms of the verb "to be" and stick *pot-* on the beginning of the ones that start with vowels, and *pos-* on the ones that start with *s*. (True, this won't work for the infinitive, but you can't have *everything*.)

Vocabulary

duo, duae, duo two
ambō, ambae, ambō both
bīnı, binae, bina two (of the same sort), a pair; two by two
glōriōsus, glōriōsa, glōriōsum fully of glory, braggart
pirus, pirī (m.) pear tree
dexter, dextera, dexterum right
mālus, mālī (m.) apple tree
sinister, sinistra, sinistrum left
pōmus, pōmī (m.) fruit tree
neuter, neutra, neutrum neither. The genitive and dative singular is irregular across the board and is considered in Chapter IV.
tertius, tertia, tertium third
vastō, vastāre to lay waste
arō, arāre to plow
habeō, habēre to have
videō, vidēre to see
currō, currere to run
agō, agere to lead; *grātiās agere* to give thanks

faciō, facere to do, make
capiō, capere to seize
veniō, venīre to come
audiō, audīre to hear
sum, esse to be
possum, posse to be able
sedeō, sedēre to sit
ad toward, to, at (with the accusative)
pirum, pirī (n.) pear. You already know about *mālum, mālī* (n.) apple.
Rōma, Rōmae (f.) Rome
propter for, because of (with the accusative)
etiam still, yet, also, even
ergō therefore
semper always
pōmārium, pōmāriī (n.) orchard
ab (before vowels), *ā* (before consonants) from (with the ablative)
pōmum, pōmī (n.) fruit

I. Translate into English

a. *Nauta sedet ad dexteram agricolārum.* (Motto of the New England Successionist Movement)
b. *Mālī pira nōn habent, sed māla.*

c. *Rōmae grātiās nōn agitis, O agricolae Galliae, propter bellum taetrum.*
d. *Triquetrum faciō agrum propter bīnōs pirōs et mālum.*
e. *Venimus ad Galliam sed nōn currimus.*
f. *Dexterum habēs; sinistrum habēs; tertium etiam habēs neutrum: ergō triquetrus es.*

II. Translate into Latin

a. Braggart sailors are always running into islands.
b. You can't see the orchard for the (fruit) trees.
c. The good adulterer gives thanks to both: to the girl *and* to the father-in-law.
d. A chamber pot is not a suitable place for a pear tree.
e. You are foul, O sons and daughters of England, not fit for a chamber pot.
f. I'm taking a couple of apples from the apple tree.

III. A Syllogism

Pōmī nōn bonī (sunt).
Mālus pōmus (est).
Mālus ergō malus (est).

CHAPTER IV

A Couple of Numbers,
A Number of Nouns

So much for the number 2. Now for the number 1 and the number 3, the only remaining cardinals below 100 that get declined in Latin. With these, and a little help from the conjunctions and quantifiers, you make any whole number you like, and then some. "One" is declined as follows:

	MASC	FEM	NEUT
NOM	ūnus	ūna	ūnum
GEN	ūnius	ūnius	ūnius
DAT	ūnī	ūnī	ūnī
ACC	ūnum	ūnam	ūnum
ABL	ūnō	ūnā	ūnō

There are essentially four other words that are declined just like *ūnus, ūna, ūnum*, and three more that are declined almost just like them. The ones that go like *ūnus, ūna, ūnum* are *ūllus, ūlla, ūllum* (any), *nūllus, nūlla, nūllum* (not any, none, no), *sōlus, sōla, sōlum* (alone, sole), and *tōtus, tōta, tōtum* (whole, all). The plurals of these are like *bonī, bonae, bona:*

NOM	sōlī	sōlae	sōla
GEN	sōlōrum	sōlārum	sōlōrum
DAT	sōlīs	sōlīs	sōlīs
ACC	sōlōs	sōlās	sōla
ABL	sōlīs	sōlīs	sōlīs

Almost the same as these are *alter, altera, alterum* (the other), *uter, utra, utrum* (which [of two]), and *neuter, neutra, neutrum* (neither [of two]).

SINGULAR

	MASC		FEM		NEUT	
NOM	alter	uter	altera	utra	alterum	utrum
GEN	alterīus	utrīus	alterīus	utrīus	alterīus	utrīus
			etc.			

This set of adjectives is doubly remarkable. First, of course, there are two traps, the genitive and dative singular case endings. Were it not for these, *ūnus, ūna, ūnum* and the others would be just so many run of the mill first-second declension adjectives. The second feature of note is that each of the adjectives of this set provides us with much the same kind of information: how many. Are we dealing with one of a kind, one of a boxed set, some, all, or none? Such words are termed quantifiers and are to the logician what metric wrenches are to the fixer of foreign cars: not quite indispensable, but far and away the best tools for the job.

If we didn't have quantifiers, we would have to make do with conjunctions. (One is reminded of the story of the farmer who wasn't sure what the plural of mongoose was and so wrote away, saying, "Send me a mongoose—in fact, make that two.") We have already encountered *et* (and), the hoary progenitor of the conjunction clan. Other conjunctions include the words for "neither . . . nor . . . ," "either . . . or . . . ," and "both . . . and . . . ."

"Neither . . . nor . . ." is straightforward enough: if you want to say "neither X nor Y (nor Z)" in Latin, you say *nec X nec Y (nec Z)* and that's all there is to it. Thus, *nec agricola nec agricolae fīlius nec fīlia agrōs arāre nōn potest* (neither the farmer nor the farmer's son nor his daughter is unable to plow the fields); *nec agricolae fīliae nec fīliō dat pōmōs nauta* (the sailor gives fruit trees to neither the farmer's daughter nor his son).

Latin distinguishes between two kinds of "either . . . or . . . ." *Aut X aut Y* means "either X or Y" where X and Y are mutually exclusive. Thus, *Marcus aut agricolae aut nautae fīlius* (Marcus is either the son of a farmer or else the son of a sailor). *Vel X vel Y* means "either X or Y" where X and Y don't automatically rule each other out. Thus, *ager idōneus vel mālīs vel pirīs* (a field suitable for either apple trees or pear trees), the implication being that the field could be used for either or both. *Ager idōneus aut mālīs aut pirīs* (a field suitable either for apple trees or else for pear trees) implies that if you plant one kind of tree, you've had it as far as the other is concerned. In the language of logic, it's the distinction between "inclusive" and "exclusive 'or's.' "

For "both . . . and . . . " the basic possibilities are these in Latin. You can use *et* or *et . . . et . . .* , as in *nauta et agricola sunt in agrō* (both the sailor and the farmer are in the field) and *et in Galliā et in Britanniā nauta nauta et matella matella* (in both Gaul and Britain, a sailor is a sailor and a chamber pot is a chamber pot). *Et* is the all-purpose joiner. Somewhat more specialized "ands" are *-que* and *atque* (sometimes known as plain *ac*). The first of these, *-que*, is an enclitic, that is, something of a linguistic parasite. The specialized task that *-que* performs is to join parts to form a whole. Thus, while *et* can join practically anything together, *-que* usually joins things which already have something to do with each other, things which complement each other. Thus, *fīliae fīliīque* (daughters and sons), *ūnus alterque* (both the one and the other). *Atque* essentially serves to emphasize the word which follows it, as in Catullus's elegy on the death of his brother, *"Frāter, Avē atque Valē"* ("Brother, Hail and Farewell").

Having considered 1, 2, and "and," and having promised to have a look at the number 3, can we put it off any longer? In fact, we can. For we can slip the third declension in first, not only on the admittedly flimsy grounds that it has the number 3 in the title, but more convincingly because "three" just so happens to be a third declension *nōmen* in Latin. Besides, you have to learn about the third declension sooner or later, and this declension has all the good words in it anyway.

Most Latin books make a big deal out of the third declension. The fact is, if you don't mind having to learn two stems per *nōmen*, a relatively small burden which you have already borne with *ager, agrī* and *taeter, taetra, taetrum* and company, the third declension is straightforward enough. The following are regular, everyday third declension nouns:

SINGULAR

NOM	pēs	mīles	homō	nōmen	iter
GEN	pedis	mīlitis	hominis	nōminis	itineris
DAT	pedī	mīlitī	hominī	nōminī	itinerī
ACC	pedem	mīlitem	hominem	nōmen	iter
ABL	pede	mīlite	homine	nōmine	itinere

PLURAL

NOM	pedēs	mīlitēs	hominēs	nōmina	itinera
GEN	pedum	mīlitum	hominum	nōminum	itinerum
DAT	pedibus	mīlitibus	hominibus	nōminibus	itineribus
ACC	pedēs	mīlitēs	hominēs	nōmina	itinera
ABL	pedibus	mīlitibus	hominibus	nōminibus	itineribus

Pēs, pedis (m.) foot; *mīles, mīlitis* (m.) soldier; *homō, hominis* (m.) man; *nōmen, nōminis* (n.) noun, name; *iter, itineris* (n.) way, journey, march.

The endings of the masculine and feminine *nōmina* of this declension are -_, *-is, -ī, -em, -e; -ēs, -um, -ibus, -ēs,* and *-ibus*. The neuter differs from these in characteristic fashion, namely, by having a different ending in the nominative and accusative cases, -_ in the singular and *-a* in the plural.

There is, alas, a hitch: these aren't the only variety of third declension *nōmina*. There are, besides these, the so-called *i* stems and mixed *i* stems.

First, the *i* stems.

42

NOM	turris	imber	animal	mare
GEN	turris	imbris	animālis	maris
DAT	turrī	imbrī	animālī	marī
ACC	turrim	(imbrem)	animal	mare
ABL	turrī	imbrī	animālī	marī

NOM	turrēs	imbrēs	animālia	maria
GEN	turrium	imbrium	animālium	marium
DAT	turribus	imbribus	animālibus	maribus
ACC	turrīs	imbrīs	animālia	maria
ABL	turribus	imbribus	animālibus	maribus

Turris, turris (f.) tower; *imber, imbris* (m.) rain; *animal, animālis* (n.) animal; *mare, maris* (n.) sea.

These differ from the "regular" third declension nouns in the following ways. Masculine and feminine nouns—of which there are so few they would hardly raise a lump under the carpet—have *i* instead of *e* in the accusative and ablative singular and in the accusative plural. They also have *-ium* instead of *-um* in the genitive plural. As is indicated by *imbrem*, the Romans didn't care much for having to keep *i* stems separate from the others and so tended to apply the *e* endings wherever they could, at least in the masculine and feminine forms. (For some reason, they didn't tamper with the neuter forms.)

It is not surprising, then, that in their eagerness to get rid of the *i* forms by replacing them with *e* forms, a hybrid should make its appearance:

NOM	urbs	nox	ūniversitās	pōns
GEN	urbis	noctis	ūniversitātis	pontis
DAT	urbī	noctī	ūniversitātī	pontī
ACC	urbem	noctem	ūniversitātem	pontem
ABL	urbe	nocte	ūniversitāte	ponte

NOM	urbēs	noctēs	ūniversitātēs	pontēs
GEN	urbium	noctium	ūniversitātium	pontium
DAT	urbibus	noctibus	ūniversitātibus	pontibus
ACC	urbīs	noctīs	ūniversitātīs	pontīs
ABL	urbibus	noctibus	ūniversitātibus	pontibus

Urbs, urbis (f.) city; *nox, noctis* (f.) night; *ūniversitās, ūniversitātis* (f.) the whole, the universe, university; *pōns, pontis* (m.) bridge.

Sometimes the genitive plural of nouns like *ūniversitās* (of which there are countless examples in Latin) leaves out the *i*; and the accusative plural is as likely as not to appear as *-ēs* across the board. The significance of this for masculine and feminine nouns is: mostly they go like *mīles* and *pēs*, mostly with *es*. Neuters sometimes go like *nōmen* and sometimes like *animal* and *mare*. The twain never meet, at least not in grammar books and dictionaries.

Adjectives of the third declension—of which "three" is one, remember—are more like *i* stems than anything else and come in three varieties: adjectives of three endings, adjectives of two endings, and adjectives of one ending. Don't get your hopes up: they're only talking about the nominative singular, and not the whole package, when they say "two" or "three" endings. Examples follow:

	MASC	FEM	NEUT
NOM	celeber	celebris	celebre
GEN	celebris	celebris	celebris
DAT	celebrī	celebrī	celebrī
ACC	celebrem	celebrem	celebre
ABL	celebrī	celebrī	celebrī

PLURAL

	MASC	FEM	NEUT
NOM	celebrēs	celebrēs	celebria
GEN	celebrium	celebrium	celebrium
DAT	celebribus	celebribus	celebribus
ACC	celebrīs	celebrīs	celebria
ABL	celebribus	celebribus	celebribus

Celeber, celebris, celebre trodden, frequented, famous.

The accusative plural of the masculine and feminine forms occasionally shows up with *-ēs* instead of *-īs.* Just as well, really, as there are already quite enough *-īs* plurals in the first and second declensions already. Otherwise, the neuter goes like *mare, maris* and the masculine and feminine go like *imber, imbris.*

Adjectives of two endings are of two kinds: comparatives and "other." Comparatives are the ones which, in English, end in -er, as in "bigger" and "better," or else have "more" in front of them, as in "more bilious," "more eccentric." To make a comparative in Latin, take the stem of one of the oblique case forms of an adjective and add *-ior* for masculine and feminine (nominative singular) and *-ius* for neuter. (This is what two endings means: one for neuter and another for all-purpose non-neuter in the nominative.) Other is other.

	MASC/FEM	NEUT	MASC/FEM	NEUT
NOM	celebrior	celebrius	implūmis	implūme
GEN	celebriōris	celebriōris	implūmis	implūmis
DAT	celebriōrī	celebriōrī	implūmī	implūmī
ACC	celebriōrem	celebrius	implūmem	implūme
ABL	celebriōre	celebriōre	implūmī	implūmī

PLURAL

	MASC/FEM	NEUT	MASC/FEM	NEUT
NOM	celebriōrēs	celebriōra	implūmēs	implūmia
GEN	celebriōrum	celebriōrum	implūmium	implūmium
DAT	celebriōribus	celebriōribus	implūmibus	implūmibus
ACC	celebriōrēs	celebriōra	implūmēs	implūmia
ABL	celebriōribus	celebriōribus	implūmibus	implūmibus

Celebrior, celebrius more famous; *implūmis, implūme* not having feathers.

So, comparatives are really to be compared with regular third declension nouns like *pēs, pedis*, while other adjectives of two endings are like the three-ending variety, only with no special nominative singular forms to keep masculine and feminine apart. *Trēs, tria* (gen. *trium*) (three) is one of these "others." Adjectives of one ending, like *pār* (gen. *paris*) (equal, even) and *atrōx* (gen. *atrōcis*) (cruel, terrible), are declined like *implūmis, implūme* and *celeber, celebris, celebre*, the only difference being that all the nominative singular forms are the same for all three genders. Again, the masculine and feminine accusative singular end in *-em* and the neuter in —, while in the plural, the nominative-accusative ending is *-ēs* for masculines and feminines and *-ia* for neuters.

And that is all there is to know about adjectives in Latin, and very nearly all there is to know about nouns.

Vocabulary

ūnus, ūna, ūnum (gen. *ūnīus*)
one

ūllus, ūlla, ūllum (gen. *ūllīus*)
any

nūllus, nūlla, nūllum (gen.
nūllīus) not any, none

sōlus, sōla, sōlum (gen. *sōlīus*)
alone, sole

tōtus, tōta, tōtum (gen. *tōtīus*)
whole, all

alter, altera, alterum (gen.
alterīus) the other

uter, utra, utrum (gen. *utrīus*)
which (of two)

neuter, neutra, neutrum (gen.
neutrīus) neither

nec . . . nec . . . neither . . .
nor . . .

aut . . . aut . . . either . . . or . . .
(excl.)

vel . . . vel . . . either . . . or . . .

et . . . et . . . both . . . and . . .

-que and

atque and

ac and

frāter, frātris (m.) brother

avē hail, hello

valē farewell, good-bye

pēs, pedis (m.) foot; *bipēs,
bipedis* having two feet

mīles, mīlitis (m.) soldier. *Mīles
glōriōsus* (the braggart

soldier) was a stock character in Roman drama.

homō, hominis (m.) man

nōmen, nōminis (n.) name,
noun

iter, itineris (n.) way, journey,
march; *iter faciō* I march,
I journey

turris, turris (f.) tower

imber, imbris (m.) shower, rain

animal, animālis (n.) animal

mare, maris (n.) sea

urbs, urbis (f.) city, walled
town

nox, noctis (f.) night

ūniversitās, ūniversitātis (f.)
universe, totality, university

pōns, pontis (m.) bridge

celeber, celebris, celebre (gen.
celebris) famous

celebrior, celebrius (gen. *cele-
briōris*) more famous. There
are basically two ways of
comparing in Latin. If you
want to say "A is more
famous than B," you can
either say *A celebrior quam
B*, with *B* in the accusative;
or you can leave out the
quam and put *B* in the ablative. Thus, *Mīles glōriōsus
celebrior quam agricolam*

47

glōriōsum and *Mīles glōriōsus celebrior agricolā glōri-
ōsō* both mean "The brag-
gart soldier is more famous
than the braggart farmer."
implūmis, implūme (gen. *implūmis*) not having feathers;
plūma, plūmae (f.) feather
trēs, tria (gen. *trium*) three
pār (gen. *paris*) equal, even,
cf. *impār* (gen. *imparis*)
unequal, odd
atrōx (gen. *atrōcis*) cruel,
terrible
mūrus, mūri (m.) wall
via, viae (f.) way, road; cf.
trivium, trivii (n.) a three-
way intersection and

quadrivium, quadrivii (n.)
a four-way intersection
gallus, galli (m.) chicken
nātūra, nātūrae (f.) nature
dicō, dicere to say
quaerō, quaerere to seek, ask
for
tunc then
respondeō, respondēre to answer
exeō, exīre to leave; the present
indicative active is: *exeō,
exīs, exit, exīmus, exitis,
exeunt.*
*dēnūdātus, dēnūdāta,
dēnūdātum* stripped; cf.
nūdus, nūda, nūdum bare
iactō, iactāre to throw

I. Translate into English

   a. *Aut imbrem super mūrōs aut pedēs mīlitum audiō in viā.*
   b. *Et gallī et porcī current in urbis taetrae viās.*
   c. *Frātrum nōmina celebria nōn sunt; nec nōmen ūnīus celebrius
      est quam nōmen alterius.*
   d. *Nātūra nec mundī sōlīus nec ūniversitātis tōtīus triquetra est.*
   e. *"Avē" dicō mīlitibus in ponte atque "Valē" agricolīs in agrō.*

II. Translate into Latin

   a. Either in the night or in the rain, you can run either into the
      tower or else into the orchard.

b. A farmer in the field and a sailor in the sea are not equal.
c. I can see the whole island from the tower and it is all foul.
d. The names of three animals are: crab, chicken, and man.
e. One man is good, the other is bad, but neither is three-cornered.

III. Read and Enjoy

Duo hominēs celebris ūniversitātis in Galliā nātūram hominis quaerunt. Ūnus alterī dīcit, "Homō sōlus animal implūme bipēs." Alter tunc non respondet, sed ab ūniversitāte exit. In nocte ad ūniversitātem venit et super mūrum ūniversitātis gallum dēnūdātum plūmīs iactat.

CHAPTER V

Questions and Answers: The Logic of the Talking Bear

There is, no doubt, a logic to the universe. The trouble with it is that it changes from time to time, from place to place, and from language to language. Fortunately, you can always ask for clarification of the rules, and it is against this very contingency that questions and answers were invented. Shortly after the invention of questions and answers, it occurred to some folk logician—possibly a Roman—to invent the shaggy dog story (*fābula canis capillīs prōmissīs*).

Shaggy dog stories, it will be recalled, are those slow-moving ones with the talking animals, beginning as often as not with a bear walking into a bar and ordering a beer and ending with the bear saying something that wouldn't be nearly so funny if it weren't being said by a bear, or possibly a pelican. What makes the shaggy dog story funny is not so much the natural dry wit of the nonhuman members of the animal kingdom as the logical whiz-bang that underlies all such stories: the everyday world has its logic and the world of talking animals has another, but the world of the shaggy dog has a third that is an uneasy combination of the two.

In this chapter, we will contemplate the logic of the Roman universe, at least to the extent of having a look at how to ask and answer several kinds of question in Latin. As an added attraction, we will also take a gander at the world of the shaggy dog and the *ursus fābulāns*, or talking bear.

It is only fitting (or unfitting or neither) that the folks who brought you the tertium quid should have three ways of asking a question to which the answer is a simple "yes" or "no." The neutral way, the one you use when you don't feel like second-guessing the person you're interrogating, involves no more than tacking -*ne* onto the word at the heart of the question. Thus, *Ursusne in tabernam introit?* (Does a *bear* go into a bar? Is a *bear* going into a bar?) and *Ursus in tabernamne introit?* (Does a bear go into a *bar*? Is a bear going into a *bar*?)

If you expect that the answer to your question is going to be "no," you have the option of suggesting as much by starting off with the word *num*, as in *Num ursī cerevisiam imperant?* (Bears don't order beer, do they?) and *Num cerevisia mala est?* (Beer isn't bad, is it?) If, on the other hand, you expect an affirmative answer, you can begin with the word *nōnne* (which is really no more than *nōn* plus *-ne*), as in *Nōnne tabernāriī cerevisiam vendunt?* (Bartenders sell beer, don't they?) and *Nōnne ursus animal implūme bipēs?* (A bear is an animal with two feet and no feathers, right?) Both *num* and *nōnne* may, of course, be used ironically: *Nōnne duōs pedēs sinistrōs habēs?* (You have two left feet, don't you?)

Latin has a number of ways of saying "yes" and "no." *Certē* (certainly), *ita* or *sīc* (thus, so), and *vērō* (in truth) are common affirmatives; *nōn* (no, not), *minimē* (not in the least), and *nūllō modō* (by no means, in no way), negatives.

Yes/no questions are of course not the only kind there are. A close relative and favorite among second-guessers is the alternative, or double, question, in which the asker offers the answerer a choice of possibilities: Are you a bear or are you a shaggy human? Appropriately enough, such questions may be phrased in a number of ways, as in the following examples. *Utrum ursus an homō capillīs prōmissīs es? Ursusne an homō capillīs prōmissīs es? Ursus an homō capillīs prōmissīs es?* In short, you can put *utrum* before the first possibility, or you can tack *-ne* onto the key word, or you can forget the whole thing and move on to the second possibility, which is generally preceded by *an*, as are all subsequent ones. A further contingency: questions which in English would end in "or not?" (Are you a bear or not?) end in *necne* in Latin (*Ursus es necne?*).

With a little imagination—and, at times, a great deal of circumlocution—it would be possible to find out just about anything by asking only yes/no questions. Happily, there is often an easier way, one involving the "Wh-" words (why, how, where, when, what, who, and the like), of which we will consider a modest sampling here. In Latin, these mostly begin with *Qu-* and work in much the same way as their English cousins: *Quārē in tabernam introīmus?* (Why are we going into a bar?), to which a plausible answer might be *Introīmus in tabernam quia cerevisiae nātūram quaerimus* (We're going into a

52

bar because we seek the nature of beer). *Quōmodō ursum salūtat tabernārius?* (How does a bartender greet a bear?), to which the answer is, clearly, *Tabernārius ursum cōmissimē salūtat* (A bartender greets a bear *very* politely).

Latin distinguishes rather more fastidiously than English among "whither" (where to?), "whence" (where from?), and just plain "where," as in *Quō eunt ursī* (Where are the bears going to?), *Unde venit cerevisia?* (Where does beer come from?), and *Ubi sunt matellae* (Where are the chamber pots?). Answers to such weighty philosophical posers as these might be: *Ursī in tabernam eunt* (The bears are going into a bar), or *Ursī ad Rōmam eunt* (The bears are going to Rome); *Cerevisia ex cūpā venit* (Beer comes out of a cask) or *Cerevisia dē tabernāriō venit* (Beer comes from a bartender); and *Matellae in Galliā sunt* (The chamber pots are in Gaul) or *Matellae sub cūpīs sunt* (The chamber pots are under the casks).

But, as the Modistae had it, *Locus nūllus nisi in tempore* (There is no place except in time), or, there's no where without a when. *Quandō* is as good a start as any—and better than most—when you want to ask "when?" *Quandō in tabernam introit ursus?* (When does a bear go into a bar?) *Quandō* can also be used in answers, such as *Ursus in tabernam introit quandō cerevisiam dēsīderat* (A bear goes into a bar when he wishes a beer).

Latin distinguishes among several "possible" times when: there is a temporal order to the universe and its contents, things have already happened, things are happening, and things are yet to happen. We have already encountered the present (active indicative) tense, the forms of the verb that are used in Latin to express what's going on now. Since there is no time like the past, we will now consider the perfect, imperfect, and pluperfect (active indicative) for good measure.

"Perfect" means finished or complete, and "imperfect," unfinished or incomplete, both from the verb *perficiō, perficere* to finish, to accomplish. The perfect tense is so called because it's used to express a completed action, as in *Ursus in tabernam introiit et cerevisiam imperāvit* (A bear went into a bar and ordered a beer).

53

The imperfect, by contrast, is used to express continuing (past) action: *Ursus in tabernam introībat et cerevisiam imperābat* (A bear was accustomed to go into a bar and order a beer or A bear was going into a bar and was ordering a beer). That is, the imperfect covers two slightly different varieties of continuing (past) action, the "I-used-to-do-this-now-and-again" kind and the "I-was-doing-this-on-such-and-such-an-occasion" kind. The pluperfect (*plus-quam-perfectum*, or, more than finished) is, as the name implies, like the perfect, only more so: it is comparable to the "I-had-done-this" tense in English.

The imperfect is the simplest of the three Latin past tenses to form:

SING	1.	imperābam	manēbam	dīcēbam
	2.	imperābās	manēbās	dīcēbās
	3.	imperābat	manēbat	dīcēbat
PLUR	1.	imperābāmus	manēbāmus	dīcēbāmus
	2.	imperābātis	manēbātis	dīcēbātis
	3.	imperābant	manēbant	dīcēbant

Imperō, imperāre to order; *maneō, manēre* to remain; *dīcō, dicere* to say.

SING	1.	faciēbam	veniēbam	eram	ībam
	2.	faciēbās	veniēbās	erās	ībās
	3.	faciēbat	veniēbat	erat	ībat
PLUR	1.	faciēbāmus	veniēbāmus	erāmus	ībāmus
	2.	faciēbātis	veniēbātis	erātis	ībātis
	3.	faciēbant	veniēbant	erant	ībant

Faciō, facere to do, make; *veniō, venīre* to come; *sum, esse* to be; *eō, īre* to go.

54

In short, the endings of the imperfect are *-bam, -bās, -bat, -bāmus,
-bātis*, and *-bant*. These are preceded by a vowel or two, depending
on the conjugation class: *ā* in verbs with infinitives in *-āre, ē* in verbs
with infinitives in *-ēre*, and *iē* in verbs with infinitives in *-īre*. Verbs
with infinitives in *-ere* with first person singular present active indicatives in *-iō*, like *faciō* and *capiō*, have *iē*, and all other *-ere* verbs
have *ē*. With verbs like *sum* and *eō*, which are wildly aberrant anyway, all bets are, of course, off.

The perfect is only slightly more complicated.

SING	1.	imperāvī	mānsī	habuī	dīxī	fēcī
	2.	imperāvistī	mānsistī	habuistī	dīxistī	fēcistī
	3.	imperāvit	mānsit	habuit	dīxit	fēcit
PLUR	1.	imperāvimus	mānsimus	habuimus	dīximus	fēcimus
	2.	imperāvistis	mānsistis	habuistis	dīxistis	fēcistis
	3.	imperāvērunt	mānsērunt	habuērunt	dīxērunt	fēcērunt

Imperō, imperāre to order; *maneō, manēre* to remain; *habeō, habēre*
to have; *dīcō, dīcere* to say; *faciō, facere* to do, make.

SING	1.	vēnī	audīvī	fuī	iī
	2.	vēnistī	audīvistī	fuistī	istī
	3.	vēnit	audīvit	fuit	iit
PLUR	1.	vēnimus	audīvimus	fuimus	iimus
	2.	vēnistis	audīvistis	fuistis	istis
	3.	vēnērunt	audīvērunt	fuērunt	iērunt

Veniō, venīre to come; *audiō, audīre* to hear; *sum, esse* to be; *eō, īre*
to go.

The endings of the perfect are *-ī, -istī, -it, -imus, -istis*, and
-ērunt. These are added to the perfect stem. How do you find out
what the perfect stem is? For verbs with infinitives in *-āre, -ēre*, and
-īre, there is a good chance that you can guess it correctly: for verbs

in *-āre* and *-īre*, take the infinitive, drop off the *-re*, and add *-v-* plus the endings. For *-ēre* verbs, take the infinitive, drop off the *-ēre*, and add *-u-* plus the endings. For all others—and for some *-ēre* and *-īre* verbs—consult the dictionary. The first person singular perfect (active indicative) is generally the third principal part given (right after the infinitive).

To make the pluperfect, take the perfect stem (*imperāv-, māns-, habu-, dīx-, fēc-, vēn-, audīv-, fu-, i-*) and add the forms of the imperfect of the verb *sum*, namely, *eram, erās, erat, erāmus, erātis, erant*. Thus: *imperāveram, imperāverās, imperāverat, imperāverāmus, imperāverātis, imperāverant*. What could be simpler, except possibly not having a pluperfect at all? But then where would we have been?

Vocabulary

fābula, fābulae (f.) a conversation, tale, story. *Fābulāre* in late Latin is "to talk" and winds up as Spanish *hablar*. *Fābulāns* (gen. *fābulantis*), talking, is an adjective of one ending, as are all present participles, of which this is one. Present participles are the ones that end in -ing in English. In Latin, present participles are nearly as easy: verbs in *-āre* have *-āns* (gen. *-antis*), as in *fābulāns* (gen. *fābulantis*); verbs in *-ēre* have *-ēns* (gen. *-entis*), as in *vidēns* (gen. *videntis*), seeing; verbs in *-īre* have *-iēns* (gen. *-ientis*), as in

audiēns (gen. *audientis*), hearing; and, as in the formation of the imperfect, verbs in *-ere* differ according as they have *-iō* or just plain *-ō* in the present: *faciēns* (gen. *facientis*) doing, making, as against *dīcēns* (gen. *dīcentis*), saying. In Latin, present participles are used in essentially two ways: *Cerevisiam imperāns, ursus* . . . (Ordering a beer, the bear . . .) and *Tabernārius cerevisiam imperantibus dat* (The bartender gives beer to the people ordering it).

canis, canis (m.) dog

capilla, capillae (f.) hair
prōmissus, prōmissa, prōmis-
  sum long, grown long, from
  the verb *prōmittō, prōmit-*
  tere to send forth
ursus, ursī (m.) bear
-ne "?"
taberna, tabernae (f.) inn,
  tavern; *tabernārius, taber-*
  nāriī (m.) innkeeper, tavernkeeper
introeō, introīre, introīvī (from
  now on, we'll give the perfect as well as the present
  and infinitive) to enter, go
  into
num "?" (I expect the answer "no")
cerevisia, cerevisiae (f.) beer
imperō, imperāre, imperāvī to
  order, command
nōnne "?" (I expect the answer
  "yes")
vendō, vendere, vendidī to sell
certē certainly
ita thus, yes
sīc thus, yes
vērō in truth
minimē not in the least
modus, modī (m.) fashion,
  way; *nūllō modō* in no way.
  The Modistae were a group
  of Latin grammarians interested in the ways of signi-
  fying.
utrum ... an ...... or ...?

necne or not?
quārē why
quia because, since
quōmodō how
salūtō, salūtāre, salūtāvī to
  greet
cōmissimē most politely
quō where to, whither
unde where from, whence
ubi where
ex, ē from, out from (with the
  ablative)
cūpa, cūpae (f.) cask
dē from, about (with the ablative)
nisi except, if not (with the
  accusative)
tempus, temporis (n.) time;
  eōdem tempore at the same
  time
quandō when
dēsiderō, dēsiderāre, dēsiderāvī
  to long for, wish for
maneō, manēre, mānsī to
  remain
perficiō, perficere, perfēcī to
  finish, complete, accomplish
trāns across (with the accusative)
pater, patris (m.) father
dominus, dominī (m.) master
  of the house, lord, em-
  ployer
cucurrit he ran (perfect of
  currō, currere)

57

respondit he answered (perfect of *respondeō, respondēre* to answer)

stultus, stulta, stultum stupid

pretium, pretiī (n.) price

sēstertium, sēstertiī (n.) 1,000 *sēstertiī*; a *sēstertius* was a silver coin worth a quarter of a *dēnārius*, which was worth ten *assēs*. An *ās* (gen. *assis*) was originally a pound of copper, but got smaller. A *sēstertium* was worth around $75.

redeō, redīre, rediī to go back

dedit he gave (perfect of *dō, dare* — that's right: *dare* — to give, the present active indicative of which is *dō, dās, dat, dāmus, dātis, dant.*

recipiō, recipere, recēpī to accept, receive

rārus, rāra, rārum rare, scarce

avis, avis (f.) bird. A *rāra avis in terrā* is as rare as hens' teeth. *terra, terrae* (f.) earth.

caritās, caritātis (f.) dearness, high price

immoderātus, immoderāta, immoderātum outrageous

I. Answer in Latin

    a. *Num ūniversitās triquetra?*
    b. *Quōmodō in duōbus locī sedēre potes eōdem tempore quandō in nūllō locō es?*
    c. *Quārē trāns viam iit gallus?*
    d. *Utrum ad dexteram an ad sinistram patris sedet?*
    e. *Ubi locus idōneus cerevisiae?*

II. Translate into Latin

    a. I was ordering a beer when the bear came into the bar.
    b. Did he say "I long for apples" or "I long for bad things"?
    c. Pears are fruits, aren't they?
    d. Where were the sailors if not in the casks?
    e. Whence have we come and whither are we going?

III. *Fābula*

Ursus in tabernam introiit et cerevisiam imperāvit. Tabernārius ex tabernā ad dominum cucurrit dīcēns, "O domine! O domine! Ursus in tabernā est et cerevisiam dēsiderat!" Dominus tabernāriō respondit, "Stulte, utrum cerevisiam an mālōs vendimus in tabernā? Ursō cerevisiam vendere potes et, quia ursī stultī sunt, dīcere potes etiam: 'Pretium sēstertium.' "

Tabernārius rediit in tabernā et ursō dedit cerevisiam dīcēns, "Pretium sēstertium." Ursus nōn respondit, sed cerevisiam recēpit. Dīxit tabernārius, fābulāns in modō tabernāriōrum, "Nōnne ursī rārae avēs in tabernā?" "Vērō," respondit ursus, "rārī sumus certē propter cerevisiae cāritātem immoderātam."

CHAPTER VI

Pronouns:
Yours, Mine, and Ours

If you were fortunate enough to be born a Roman male, you could count on being issued three names for free: a *praenōmen*, much like our first name; a *nōmen*, which was the name of your *gēns* (clan); and a *cōgnōmen*, your family name, comparable to our last name. To this last might later be added an *āgnōmen*, a sort of honorific nickname. (For this you had to do something, like be from Africa or topple the government.)

If you chanced to be born a Roman female, you didn't make out nearly as well in the name department as in most others in Roman society. If you were the first daughter in the family, you got to have the feminine-gender form of your father's *nōmen*, and that was essentially that. If you were the second (or succeeding) daughter, you not only got to have the feminine-gender form of your father's *nōmen*, you also got a number to stick on after it: The Second (or Third, or Nth), all depending on how many older sisters you had. Thus, Pūblia Duodecima would have been the unhappy twelfth daughter of some prolific male of the *gēns* Pūblius. To this, a Roman female could add the genitive form of her husband's name.

Fortunately, even the most drably named Roman had her personal *prōnōmen*, or pronoun. Well, so did everybody else, and the number of *different* personal pronouns available for general use was, to put it mildly, small. But at least when Pūblia Duodecima said, "*Ego . . . ,*" she could rest assured that everybody listening would know precisely whom she meant.

The Latin personal pronouns for the first and second persons are declined below. (The third person will be considered by himself, herself, itself, and themselves in Chapter IX.)

FIRST PERSON

	SINGULAR	PLURAL
NOM	ego	nōs
GEN	meī	nostrum, nostrī
DAT	mihi	nōbis
ACC	mē	nōs
ABL	mē	nōbis

NOM	tū	vōs
GEN	tuī	vestrum, vestrī
DAT	tibi	vōbīs
ACC	tē	vōs
ABL	tē	vōbīs

Ego, meī I; *tū, tūī* you.

Wildly irregular personal pronouns have always been a specialty of the Indo-European family. You'd think that it would have occurred to somebody by now to make the system regular and therefore easier for everybody to learn. Actually, most of the Indo-European languages *have* undergone some changes in that direction, but virtually always at the expense of the few regularities of the original system. The Latin personal pronouns are just such a story.

Consider, for example, how regular-looking the genitive singulars *meī* and *tuī* are. Their *-ī* ending must be none other than our old friend from the second declension. (In no other respects, of course, are *ego* and *tū* declined like second declension forms, but you can't have everything.) The genitive plurals *nostrum* and *vestrum* have the right ending for the genitive plural forms of the third declension, but their stems look suspiciously different from the others in the paradigm. Not only that, the endings of the dative and ablative plurals *nōbīs* and *vōbīs* look more like *second* declension than third. The alternate forms *nostrī* and *vestrī* seem to have the genitive *singular* ending of the second declension, as well as the peculiar stems. No better from this side than that.

As it happens, *nostrī* and *vestrī* are less bizarre than *nostrum* and *vestrum*. *Nostrum* and *vestrum* were created by taking *nostrī* and *vestrī* and replacing their genitive singular ending *-ī* with the "more reasonable-looking" genitive plural ending *-um* from the third declension. (*Somebody* must have thought it looked or at least sounded more reasonable.) As for *nostrī* and *vestrī*, like *meī* and *tuī*, these were originally not *personal* pronoun forms but, rather, the genitive singular masculine/neuter forms of the *possessive* pronouns:

62

FIRST PERSON SINGULAR (MY)   FIRST PERSON PLURAL (OUR)

SINGULAR

	MASC	FEM	NEUT	MASC	FEM	NEUT
NOM	meus	mea	meum	noster	nostra	nostrum
GEN	meī	meae	meī	nostrī	nostrae	nostrī
DAT	meō	meae	meō	nostrō	nostrae	nostrō
ACC	meum	meam	meum	nostrum	nostram	nostrum
ABL	meō	meā	meō	nostrō	nostrā	nostrō

PLURAL

	MASC	FEM	NEUT	MASC	FEM	NEUT
NOM	meī	meae	mea	nostrī	nostrae	nostra
GEN	meōrum	meārum	meōrum	nostrōrum	nostrārum	nostrōrum
DAT	meīs	meīs	meīs	nostrīs	nostrīs	nostrīs
ACC	meōs	meās	mea	nostrōs	nostrās	nostra
ABL	meīs	meīs	meīs	nostrīs	nostrīs	nostrīs

Tuus, tua, tuum, the second person singular "your," is declined in the same way as *meus, mea, meum; vester, vestra, vestrum*, the second person plural "your," in the same way as *noster, nostra, nostrum*.

What, you might well ask, are possessive pronouns, and what are they doing in among the personal pronouns? Possessive pronouns are really adjectives whose sole purpose is to tell you who owns the nouns that they modify (and with which they agree in number, gender, and case, in the manner of all other self-respecting Latin adjectives): thus, *clepsydra mea* (my water clock), *calceus noster* (our shoe). If the possessive pronouns are really adjectives, why are they called pronouns, and not something more reasonable, like adjectives? The reason is not so much that grammarians are perverse (although they may be), nor even that adjectives were long considered to be just another kind of noun (*nōmen*) and nobody has gotten around to reclassifying them yet. The real reason has to do with the nature of pronouns.

63

Literally, a *prōnōmen* is a word that you can use in place of a *nōmen*. This means among other things that a pronoun can be used in place of a noun. For example, if I'm talking to my friend George, I'm not obliged to say, "Hi, George. What's George been up to lately? Does George still like George's job?" and so on, all this while looking George squarely in the eye. Thanks to the personal pronouns, I can omit as many of these "Georges" as I wish, substituting the appropriate form of the second person singular pronoun "you."

The appropriate form of "you" for "George's job" would be the genitive, the rule of thumb being that when one noun possesses another, the possessor appears in the genitive case: thus, *calceus piscātōris* (the fisherman's shoe) and *piscātor auctōris* (the author's fisherman). Now, you might expect that since personal pronouns stand in for nouns, possession would be expressed by the genitive case forms of the personal pronouns, thereby rendering the invention of the possessive pronouns—words which essentially fill in for the genitive case forms of the personal pronouns, which are themselves filling in for nouns—quite unnecessary. As it so happened, the possessive pronouns prospered and the original genitive forms of the personal pronouns were given their gold watches and were never heard of again.

This retirement was actually a bit hasty, for the genitive case did have other uses besides the expression of ownership. One such use shows up in constructions of the *amor mātris* type. *Amor mātris* can mean either of two things: "love of mother," in the sense of either "mother's love," or "love *for* mother." "Love of mother" of the first variety is called a subjective genitive because "mother" is the originator and presumptive dispensor of the love in question. "Love of mother" of the second type is called an objective genitive because "mother" is the object of the affection. These two varieties of love can be quite unambiguously expressed in Latin through the use of possessive pronouns in the first instance and personal pronouns in the second: *amor tuus* ("your love" for somebody or something), *propter amōrem tuum* ("because of your love" for somebody or something); but *amor tibi* (somebody's "love for you"), *propter amōrem tuī* (because of [somebody's] love for you).

Vocabulary

praenōmen, praenōminis (n.) first name

nōmen, nōminis (n.) name (of the *gēns*), noun

gēns, gentis (f.) clan, race, people

cōgnōmen, cōgnōminis (n.) family name, last name

āgnōmen, āgnōminis (n.) honorific surname

ego, meī I

nōs, nostrum (nostrī) we

tū, tuī you (singular)

vos, vestrum (vestrī) you (plural)

meus, mea, meum my

noster, nostra, nostrum our

tuus, tua, tuum your (belonging to you, singular)

vester, vestra, vestrum your, belonging to you (plural)

clepsydra, clepsydrae (f.) water clock

calceus, calceī (m.) shoe which, unlike the more frequently depicted sandal — *solea, soleae* (f.) — which covered only the sole of the foot, covered the whole foot

piscātor, piscātōris (m.) fisherman; cf. *piscis, piscis* (m.) fish

amor, amōris (m.) love; cf. *amō, amāre, amāvī* to love; and *amīcus, amīcī* (m.), *amīca, amīcae* (f.) friend

māter, mātris (f.) mother

Morbōnia, Morbōniae (f.) Plagueville; cf. *morbus, morbī* (m.) a distemper; and *abīre Morbōniam* to go to hell

mercātor, mercātōris (m.) merchant

valedīcō, valedīcere, valedīxī to say farewell

Sicilia, Siciliae (f.) Sicily

priōre annō last year; cf. *prior, prius* (gen. *priōris*) former, prior; and *annus, annī* (m.) year

cīvitās, cīvitātis (f.) a community of citizens, a city; cf. *cīvis, cīvis* (m.) citizen

cum when, since; *cum* also means "with" and takes the ablative

ī go (imperative). The imperative is the form of the verb that you use to order people around (cf. *imperō, imperāre* to order). In Latin, the active imperative is made as follows: to order one person to do something, take the infinitive of the verb in question and lop off the *-re*, as in *Cerevisiam imperā!* (Order a beer!), *Vidē supra* (See above), *Vende ursō cerevisiam!* (Sell the bear a beer!), *Cape cerevisiam!* (Seize the beer!), and *Audī mihi!* (Hear me, i.e., listen to me!). There are a few exceptions from the *-ere* class, like *dīc* (say!) and *fac* (do, make!). The way you order more than one person at a time is to add *-te* to the form of the singular imperative for *-āre*, *-ēre*, and *-ire* verbs—*imperāte, vidēte, audīte*—and, in *-ere* verbs take the infinitive, lop off the *-ere*, and add *-ite*—*vendite, capite, dīcite, facite.*

pulcher, pulchra, pulchrum pretty

forum, forī (n.) marketplace, public square

stō, stāre, stetī to stand; sometimes *stō, stāre* is used to mean "to be"

fōrmōsissimus, fōrmōsissima, fōrmōsissimum most beautiful; cf. *fōrmōsus, fōrmōsa, fōrmōsum* beautiful. Such adjectives as *fōrmōsissimus*, etc., are called superlatives and are made by taking the oblique (non-nominative singular) stem of an adjective and adding *-issimus, -issima*, and *-issimum*.

antiquus, antīqua, antīquum old, ancient

nāvis, nāvis (f.) ship

gubernātor, gubernātōris (m.) helmsman (which eventually works its way into English as "governor")

dēscendō, dēscendere, dēscendī to descend, get down

ut mihi nārrāvit or so he told me; cf. *nārrō, nārrāre, nārrāvī* to make known, narrate. We'll talk about *ut* in the next chapter.

perveniō, pervenīre, pervēnī to arrive, reach

mīrābile vīsū marvelous to see; cf. *mīrābile dictū* marvelous to say

horam VII mōnstrat it says
seven o'clock; hōra, hōrae
(f.) hour; mōnstrō, mōn-
strāre, mōnstrāvī to show,
make plain
rogō, rogāre, rogāvī to ask
hōram eandem minimē mōn-
strant they don't tell the
same time; they tell the
same time not at all

opus est nōbīs duābus clepsydrīs we need two water
clocks; literally, there is a
need to us for two water
clocks, "us" being in the
dative and "for two water
clocks" being in the ablative
sine without (with the ablative)
ecce behold

I. Fābula: "Dē Duābus Clepsydrīs Morbōniae"

Mercātōrī valedīcēbat amīcus. "Ego in Siciliā eram priōre annō, in
Morbōniā, cīvitāte gentis meae; cum facis iter tuum ad Siciliam ī
ad cīvitātem gentis meae. Tōta pulchra est, atque in forō stat
fōrmōsissima et antīqua clepsydra."
    Mercātor nāve ad Siciliam trānsiit et gubernātōrī dīxit, "Dēsīderō
ego in cīvitātem amīcī meī dēscendere, quia stat in forō clepsydra
antīqua atque pulchra, ut mihi nārrāvit."
    Ita ad forum cīvitātis Morbōniae pervēnit: mīrābile vīsū, nōn
erat clepsydra sōla sed duae! Ūna hōram VII, altera hōram VI
mōnstrat. Mercator in tabernam introiit et tabernāriō rogāvit,
"Quārē in forō duae clepsydrae stant? Quārē aut hōram VII bīnae
nōn mōnstrant, aut hōram VI nōn mōnstrant ambae?" Respondit
mercātōrī tabernārius, "Quia hōram eandem minimē mōnstrant,
opus est nōbīs etiam duābus clepsydrīs."

II. Translate into English

   a. Estne tuum Āfricānus āgnōmen an cōgnōmen Āfricānus
      vestrum?

b. *In cīvitāte nostrā stat clepsydra, sed nec fōrmōsa nec pulchra est.*

c. *Ō stulte! Pervēnisti ad cīvitātem gentis nostrae sine calceōs tuōs!*

d. *Ecce tū pulchra es, amica mea! Ecce tū pulchra es!* (*Song of Songs*)

e. *Quia fēcistis mihi bona, vōbīs clepsydram nostram dō.*

III. Translate into Latin

a. I said farewell to my ancient water clock in Morbonia last year.
b. You need a helmsman, my friends.
c. Why did the fisherman give your shoes to me?
d. You alone are my friend, o bartender.
e. Both of your cities need a water clock, my love!

CHAPTER VII

Mood Music

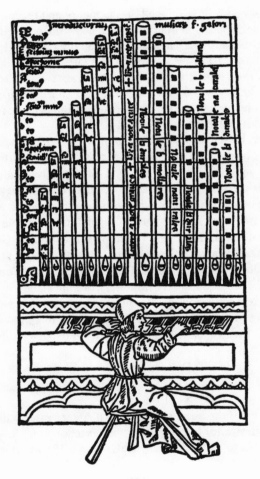

About pre-Christian Roman music we know virtually nothing, since it did not apparently occur to any Roman musicologist to take the time to write the definitive treatise on modern music or even to review the latest on the Roman Top Ten. One suspects that if the Romans had Bach or the Beatles, they were Greek.

The first real light to be shed on the theory and practice of Roman music appears in the Dark Ages, when the people in the treatise-writing business had theories for all occasions and music—or "good" music at least—was analyzed to a fare-thee-well along with practically everything else. One of the more noteworthy treatise-writers of the day was Guido d'Arezzo, who flourished around A.D. 1000 and who gave us a good first version of the names of the notes of the (major) scale: do-re-mi-fa-sol-la-ti-do.

Actually, his names went "*ut-re-mi-fa-sol-la*" and stopped. The reason why he quit after six instead of going the full eight that we now know and love is that, in the good old days, they had a different strategy for measuring out musical space than the one they use now. We use the octave (the distance between one frequency and two times that frequency) as our musical "foot" and we divide it into twelve equally spaced "inches" (semitones) accordingly. Guido and his associates operated with something called the "hexachord," an acoustic ruler divided as follows: Tone Tone Semitone Tone Tone (where one Tone equals two Semitones), or nine inches by our current system of reckoning. By some judicious fiddling with the ruler, you can move from one measuring system to another without too much difficulty, deriving the octave from two overlapping hexachords:

Do-Re-Mi-Fa-Sol-La-Ti-Do (-Re-Mi . . .)
  T T S T T
              T T S (T T . . .)

The names of the notes according to d'Arezzo made a nifty mnemonic device for learning all about hexachords: *Ut-Re-Mi-Fa-Sol-La* happen to be the initial syllables in the first six lines of a

hymn in which each musical line begins one note higher in the
hexachord than the last:

Ut *queant laxīs*
Resonāre *fibrīs*
Mīra *gestōrum*
Famulī *tuōrum*
Solve *pollutī[s]*
Labiī[s] *reātum*
    Sāncte Joannes.

"In order that with unrestrained hearts your servants might be able
to sing the wonders of your acts, remove the sin from their polluted
lips, Saint John." Note the two different uses of the ablative: *laxīs
fibrīs* is an example of the so-called ablative of means; *pollutī[s]
labiī[s]* , of the ablative of separation.

    The relatively unsingable syllable *ut* was soon replaced by the
vastly more mellifluous *do* (as in *dominus*) to everyone's satisfaction.
But *ut* was and remained to the last down-home Latin gasp a very
handy word, as may be inferred from a glance at the customary
several columns devoted to its definition and use in the dictionary.
Let us have a closer look.
    Ut, in its meaning of "as," has already been met in *ut mihi
narrāvit* (or so he told me), to which may be compared *Ut ursus
cerevisiam dēsīderat lupus* (Like the bear, the wolf wants a beer)
and *Ut cum ursīs, ita cum lupīs hominibusque cerevisiā* (as with
bears, so it is with wolves and men in the matter of beer, in which
cerevisiā exemplifies the ablative of specification). All sorts of
changes may be rung on *ut* as "as," but its primary importance is in
its meaning of "in order that, in the hope that, would that," as in
Ut queant (In order that they might be able) and *Ut Morbōniam
abeās!* (Would that you would go to hell!) When *ut* appears under its
"would that" or "in order that" hat, the verbs that follow it appear
in the subjunctive mood.

71

Subjunctive mood? For all practical purposes, this means special verb forms in four tenses: the present, imperfect, perfect, and pluperfect. The present goes as follows:

	1.	imperem	maneam	dīcam
SING	2.	imperēs	maneās	dīcās
	3.	imperet	maneat	dīcat
	1.	imperēmus	maneāmus	dīcāmus
PLUR	2.	imperētis	maneātis	dīcātis
	3.	imperent	maneant	dīcant

Imperō, imperāre to order; *maneō, manēre* to remain; *dīcō, dīcere* to say.

	1.	faciam	audiam	sim	eam
SING	2.	faciās	audiās	sīs	eās
	3.	faciat	audiat	sit	eat
	1.	faciāmus	audiāmus	sīmus	eāmus
PLUR	2.	faciātis	audiātis	sītis	eātis
	3.	faciant	audiant	sint	eant

Faciō, facere to do, make; *audiō, audīre* to hear; *sum, esse* to be; *eō, īre* to go.

For all but a very few utterly off-the-wall irregular verbs, you form the present subjunctive in the following way: for non-*āre* verbs, take the first person singular present active indicative form, i.e., the first principle part, remove the *-ō* and add *-am, -ās, -at, -āmus, -ātis, -ant*; and for *-āre* verbs, since they have plenty of *a*s already, take the first principle part, remove the *-ō* and add *-em, -ēs, -et, -ēmus, -ētis, -ent*—that is, the same endings as the others but with *e* (*ē*) instead of *a* (*ā*).

On to the imperfect subjunctive, which goes as follows:

SING	1.	imperārem	manērem		dīcerem
	2.	imperārēs	manērēs		dīcerēs
	3.	imperāret	manēret		dīceret
PLUR	1.	imperārēmus	manērēmus		dīcerēmus
	2.	imperārētis	manērētis		dīcerētis
	3.	imperārent	manērent		dīcerent

SING	1.	facerem	audīrem	essem	īrem
	2.	facerēs	audīrēs	essēs	īrēs
	3.	faceret	audīret	esset	īret
PLUR	1.	facerēmus	audīrēmus	essēmus	īrēmus
	2.	facerētis	audīrētis	essētis	īrētis
	3.	facerent	audīrent	essent	īrent

What could be more regular?

To make the imperfect subjunctive, take the infinitive (the second principle part), lop off the final *-e* and add *-em, -ēs, -et, -ēmus, -ētis, -ent*, which happen to be the present subjunctive endings for *-āre* verbs (see above), so they are no trouble to learn, or not much.

To form the subjunctive of the perfect and pluperfect, take the first person singular perfect active indicative (the third principal part), remove the *-ī*, and add endings. For the perfect subjunctive, these are: *-erim, eris, -erit, erimis, eritis, -erint,* as in *imperāverim, imperaveris, imperāverit, imperaverimus, imperaveritis, imperāverint* and *dīxerim, dīxeris, dīxerit, dīxerimus, dīxeritis, dīxerint.* The endings of the pluperfect subjunctive are *-issem, -issēs, -isset, -issēmus, -issētis, -issent,* as in *imperāvissem, imperāvissēs, imperāvisset, imperāvissēmus, imperāvissētis, imperāvissent* and *dīxissem, dīxissēs, dīxisset, dīxissēmus, dīxissētis, dīxissent.* Or you could say that the pluperfect subjunctive is made by taking the perfect stem and adding first *-iss-* and then the endings of the present subjunctive of *-āre* verbs. The pluperfect subjunctive of *eō, īre* (to go), whose perfect stem is *ī-*, is *īssem, īssēs, īsset, īssēmus, īssētis, īssent.*

What, exactly, is the subjunctive mood and how is it used? Latin has three "moods," that is, manners of expressing action: the indicative, the subjunctive, and the imperative. The imperative, as already suggested, is used for giving commands: Listen to me! (*Audī mihi!*). The indicative is used for making statements and asking questions: You are listening to me (*Audīs mihi*), Are you listening to me? (*Audīsne mihi?*). The subjective has functions which are *like* those of both the imperative and the indicative. For example, the subjunctive is customarily used to express a wish: Would that (I wish that) you would listen to me (*Ut audiās mihi*), not as blunt as a command nor an out-and-out accusation of inattention. Similarly, I'm coming so that (in the hope that) you might listen to me (*Veniō ut audiās mihi*).

The subjunctive is also used to express doubt or vague possibility: Perhaps he is speaking badly of you (*Forsitan malē tē dīcat*). Again, this is weaker than a direct accusation in which the indicative would be used: *Malē tē dīcit.*

So far, all our examples have come from the present tense. This is not to imply that you can't express lingering doubt about a past event or that you can't wish that something had turned out differently. Both are possible and both generally require the subjunctive. For example, Maybe he went into a cave and not a bar (*Forsitan in spēluncam et nōn in tabernam introierit*); Would that (I wish that) they had given me your water clock (*Utinam clepsydram tuam dedissent mihi*); or If only I had arrived more speedily (*O sī celerius pervēnissem*).

"If only" brings us to the last use of the subjunctive that will be considered here, namely, in conditions contrary to fact. The implication of "If only I had arrived more speedily" is that something which happened as a result of my dawdling wouldn't have or at least might not have. For example, If I had arrived more speedily, they would have left sooner (*Sī celerius pervēnissem, mātūrius exissent*), or If I were a bear, I would be a talking bear (*Sī ursus essem, ursus fābulāns essem*). Both subjunctives in the first example are pluperfect, which are the appropriate ones for talking about conditions contrary to fact in the past—if such and such had happened (which it didn't), then such and such else would have happened (which it didn't). Both subjunctives in the second example are imperfect, this being the appropriate tense for talking about conditions contrary to fact in the present—if such were happening now (which it isn't), then such and such else would happen (which it isn't). The present subjunctive in contrary-to-fact conditions is reserved for conditions which, if they aren't actually contrary to fact, are in the realm of idle speculation—if such and such should happen in the future, then such and such else might happen, but it's none too clear that any such thing will in fact happen. We will consider the subjunctive further in the next chapter when we discuss the last of the active indicative forms, the future and future perfect.

Vocabulary

ut as, in order that, would that. To say "in order that ... not" or "would that ... not," you use *nē*, as in *Ut in ūniversitātem eat nē agrōs vastet!* (Let him go to college so that he may not waste the fields!)

queō, quīre, quiī to be able (conjugated like *eō, īre, iī*)

laxus, laxa, laxum relaxed, unrestrained

resonō, resonāre, resonāvī to resound

fibra, fibrae (f.) fiber, entrails

mīrus, mīra, mīrum wonderful, amazing

gesta, gestōrum (n.) deeds, acts; *gesta, gestōrum* is a *plūrāle tantum*, that is, something that only appears in the plural.

famulus, famulī (m.) servant

solveō, solvēre, solvī to loosen, free, dissolve

pollūtus, pollūta, pollūtum fouled

labia, labiōrum (n.) lips; another *plūrāle tantum*

reātus, reātūs (f.) sin, charge; this is a fourth declension noun (see Chapter XI).

sānctus, sāncta, sānctum sacred

lupus, lupī (m.) wolf; the person who appears while being discussed is *lupus in fābulā.*

forsitan perhaps

malē badly; adverbs in Latin are easy: take a first-second declension adjective, like *malus, mala, malum*, lop off the ending and add *-ē*. For third declension adjectives, take the oblique case stem, like *celebr-*, and add *-iter* (*celebriter* famously). The only "regular" adverbs which aren't formed in this way are ones like *sapienter* (knowingly), which are made from present participles, like *sapiēns* (gen. *sapientis*) (knowing). With these, plain *-er* is added to the oblique case stem.

spēlunca, spēluncae (f.) cave

utinam would that; *utinam* is used in place of plain *ut* in the past

sī if

celerius more speedily; this may look like the neuter nominative-accusative singular comparative form of the adjective *celer, celeris, celere* (speedy). The fact is, the nominative-accusative neuter form of the comparative of the adjective and the comparative of the adverb are made the same way in Latin (with the customary one or two exceptions): take the oblique case stem and add *-ius*.

mātūrius earlier

crescō, crescere, crēvī to grow, increase; Latin has a number of verbs ending in *-scō*, called inceptives or inchoatives. In PIE, these *-scō* verbs had the sense of "to begin to" something, e.g., begin to grow.

ōs, ōris (n.) mouth

diūtius for a while longer, for a longer time; this is the comparative to *diū* (for a long time).

avia, aviae (f.) grandmother

barba, barbae (f.) beard

avus, avī (m.) grandfather

silvāticus, silvātica, silvāticum forest-dwelling, wild; cf. *silva, silvae* (f.) forest

frīgus, frīgoris (n.) the cold

nix, nivis (f.) snow

mensis, mensis (m.) month

trānscēdō, trānscēdere, trāns-
cessī to go by, pass
famescō, famescere, —— to
become hungry; cf. *famēs,*
famis (f.) hunger, and
famēlicus, famēlica, famēli-
cum famished
quoque too, also
bōs, bovis (m., f.) ox, cow
cibus, cibī (m.) food
adferō, adferre, attulī to bring
back; *ferō* in its various
forms is a very popular number in Latin. The present
indicative active: *ferō, fers,*
fert, ferimus, feritis, ferunt;
the imperfect indicative
active: *ferēbam, ferēbās,*
etc.; perfect indicative active: *tulī, tulistī,* etc.; pluperfect indicative active:
tuleram, tulerās, etc.; present subjunctive active:
feram, ferās, etc.; imperfect
subjunctive active: *ferrem,*
ferrēs, etc.; perfect subjunctive active: *tulerim, tuleris,*
etc.; pluperfect subjunctive

active: *tulissem, tulissēs,*
etc.
euge! Great! Right on!
serpēns, serpentis (m.) snake,
crawling animal; cf. *serpō,*
serpere, serpsī to creep,
crawl
sors, sortis (f.) lot, chance;
sortēs dūcere to cast lots
(*dūcere* is conjugated like
dīcere)
cervus, cervī (m.) deer
lēgō, lēgāre, lēgāvī to delegate,
appoint; cf. *lēgātus, lēgātī*
(m.) delegate, lieutenant
turtur, turturis (m.) turtledove,
turtle
tenebrae, tenebrārum (f.)
shadows, darkness; another
plūrāle tantum
nōnnūllus, nōnnūlla, nōnnūllum
(gen. *nōnnūllius*) some,
several
ūnā as one, together, at once
prope near (with the accusative)
vōx, vōcis (f.) voice

I. Translate into Latin

   a. If only they had had a chamber pot!
   b. He may be a man or he may not be (i.e., he may well turn out
      to be a man or he may not), but I wish he would leave my
      tavern!

c. If an apple tree should grow in your mouth, you would no longer have a mouth but an orchard.
d. If grandma had a beard, she'd be grandpa.
e. If the bear hadn't wanted a beer, he wouldn't have come into the bar.

II. *Fābula*

Animālia silvātica diū in spēluncā manēbant propter frīgus atque nivem immoderātam. Mēnsis trānscessit et animālia famescēbant. "Famēlicus ego," dīxit ursus. "Ego quoque," dīxit bōs. Dīxit lupus, "Exeat ūnus ut cibum nōbīs adferat." "Euge!" respondit serpēns, "Tū forsitan dēsiderēs īre ut cibum adferās?" "Minimē!" respondit alter. "Sortēs dūcāmus," dīxit cervus, "ut lēgātum lēgēmus." Ita sorte turturem lēgāvērunt.

Valedīxit animālibus turtur et in tenebrās spēluncae abiit. Nōnnūllae hōrae trānscessērunt et rogāvit ursus, "Ubi turtur? Famēlicōsus sum!" "Ego quoque," dīxit bōs. "Turtur diūtissimē abiit. O sī lēgāvissēmus celeriōrem," dīxērunt ūnā lupus serpēnsque. Tunc ē tenebrīs prope protam spēluncae vōcem turturis audīvērunt: "O amīcī, sī ita malē mē dīcātis, hīc in spēluncā maneam."

CHAPTER VIII

The Future

It is not everybody who can tell you something about the future and have it turn out to be true. The original Indo-Europeans, rather than make frequent liars of each other, seem to have decided that the safest way of talking about the future was in the subjunctive, and a separate future tense could wait to be invented until later when life was bound to be more certain. Or so it seems to have happened, for not only is the future expressed in nearly as many different ways as there are attested Indo-European languages, suggesting that each has had to shift for itself, but in many cases, one Indo-European's future is another's subjunctive, or something suspiciously like it.

Another trout in the milk is that the future (and future perfect) usually turns out, in languages which still have a subjunctive, to be the one tense of the indicative that doesn't have a corresponding set of subjunctive forms.

Latin appears to have had some difficulty making up its mind as to how to make the future tense from the various parts at hand, and so has opted for two different ways, one for the *-āre* and *-ēre* verbs and another for the *-ere* and *-īre* verbs:

		-āre	-ēre	-ere	-īre
	1.	rogābō	manēbō	dīcam	faciam
SING	2.	rogābis	manēbis	dīcēs	faciēs
	3.	rogābit	manēbit	dīcet	faciet
	1.	rogābimus	manēbimus	dīcēmus	faciēmus
PLUR	2.	rogābitis	manēbitis	dīcētis	faciētis
	3.	rogābunt	manēbunt	dīcent	facient

Rogō, rogāre to ask; *maneō, manēre* to remain; *dīcō, dīcere* to say; *faciō, facere* to do, make.

		veniam	feram	erō	ībō
SING	1.	veniam	feram	erō	ībō
	2.	veniēs	ferēs	eris	ībis
	3.	veniet	feret	erit	ībit
	1.	veniēmus	ferēmus	erimus	ībimus
PLUR	2.	veniētis	ferētis	eritis	ībitis
	3.	venient	ferent	erunt	ībunt

Veniō, venīre to come; *ferō, ferre* to bring, carry; *sum, esse* to be; *eō, īre* to go.

The future of the *-ere* and *-īre* verbs is just like their present subjunctive, except that in all forms but the first person singular, where the subjunctive has *a* (*ā*), the future has *e* (*ē*), something which has made for several millennia of confusion. (Did he say he *might* do it or did he say he really *would*? *Utrum "faciam" dīxit an "faciam"?*) The future of the -*āre* and -*ēre* verbs has never been in doubt, though people have been known to confuse it with the imperfect.

There are more elaborate ways to talk about the future in Latin than with the future tense (for situations in which a confident prediction can be made) or the subjunctive (for the more cautious readings of entrails). These ways mostly involve the use of participles, of which Latin has an impressive supply.

The present participle can be used in what is at least technically a future sense: Seeing the bear, the bartender will greet us quite politely (*Ursum vidēns, tabernārius cōmissimē nōs salūtābit*). The alternative—or *an* alternative anyway—would be to say, When he sees the bear (literally, when he shall see the bear), the bartender will greet us quite politely (*Cum ursum vidēbit, tabernārius cōmissimē nōs salūtābit*).

The past participle can be pressed into similar service, but this takes a little more finesse. First, of course, it helps to know what one is. In English, the past participle is what comes right after the verb "to have" in "The turtle has *vanished*," "He had *eaten* a mushroom," "Having *eaten* the mushroom, he vanished," "Having *vanished*, the turtle then made good his escape," "The turtle has *been* away for a long time," and the like. It also shows up after the verb "to be" in passive constructions (where the subject always winds up being acted upon by somebody who may not even be in the sentence), like "A mushroom was *eaten*," "A mushroom has been *eaten*," "Having been *eaten*, the mushroom was no longer visible." Sometimes, it shows up all by itself disguised as an adjective, as in "The *eaten* mushroom is no longer visible" or "The *chosen* few are too many." It's worth noting that the sense of these constructions with noun modified by past participle is always passive: the *eaten* mushroom was obviously *eaten by* somebody, the *chosen* few were *chosen by* somebody.

Not for nothing is the Latin past participle known as the perfect *passive* participle: in Latin, you only get past participles of the "chosen" and "eaten" variety, that is, to verbs which can be used passively: *be* chosen, *be* eaten. (A verb like *ēvānescō, ēvānescere*, to vanish, would never have a past participle in Latin because you can't *be* vanished in Latin any more than you can in English. Being chosen and, heaven forbid, eaten is another story entirely.)

The way you make the past participle in Latin is to look up the verb in question and note its fourth (and, you will be pleased to know, final) principal part. This should end in either *-tum* or *-sum* and is called the supine, whose characteristics will be discussed in Chapter XI. (If the fourth principal part ends in *-ūrus*, hastily close the dictionary and forget what you have seen: this is an imposter whose presence tells you that the verb in question doesn't have a past participle.) Lop off the *-um* and add the endings for adjectives of the *bonus, bona, bonum* variety. Thus, *lēgō, lēgāre, lēgāvī, lēgātum* (to delegate, appoint) has *lēgātus, lēgāta, lēgātum* (delegated, appointed) as its past participle, and *edō, ēsse, ēdī, ēssum* (to eat) has *ēssus, ēssa, ēssum* (eaten). Note: just because a verb has a fourth principal part that ends in *-tum* or *-sum*, that doesn't automatically give you license to make past participles from it; the verb *has* to be of the sort that can be used passively.

There is a shortcut to the fourth principal part of at least some kinds of verbs that allows you to bypass the dictionary. (Any shortcut to the fourth principal part can easily be converted to an even shorter cut to the past participle, as you have no doubt already observed, but we'll plug along on the middle path because the fourth principal part is good to know about, as it serves as the base for a number of different parts of speech.) The *-āre* and *-īre* verbs regularly form the supine (the fourth principal part) by dropping the *-re* of the infinitive and adding *-tum*, as in *salūtātum* from *salūtāre* and *audītum* from *audīre*. Some *-ēre* verbs work this way too, though some drop the *-ēre* as a whole and add *-itum* instead, and still others do even stranger things. For *-ēre* verbs, you might well check the dictionary. The *-ere* verbs generally drop the *-ere* and add *-tum* and that's all there is to it, except for some minor phonetic adjustments. Thus, *factum* from *facere*, but *actum* from *agō, agere*, or *versum* from *vertō, vertere* (to turn). The *-ere* verbs, like the *-ēre* verbs, don't always work the way they're supposed to, but no language is perfect.

The past participle can be used to express the future in the following way: The mushroom having been eaten, the turtle will vanish (*Fungō ēssō, turtur ēvānēscet*). For the rather cumbersome "The mushroom having been eaten," read "When the mushroom has been eaten" or "With the mushroom eaten." This construction, made from a noun and a past participle in the ablative, is called an ablative absolute and was an old favorite among the Romans. (Actually, you can make an ablative absolute with two nouns: *Turture agricolā, rārō edēmus*, With the turtle as farmer, that is, as long as the turtle is farmer, we will seldom eat.)

There are two more participial possibilities in Latin, both of which get used to talk about the future. One of these, the future participle, is essentially active in meaning, while the other, the gerundive, is essentially passive. The future participle is made by taking the fourth principal part, if it ends in *-tum* or *-sum*, removing the *-um* and adding *-ūr* plus the endings for adjectives of the *bonus, bona, bonum* type. This *-ūr* happens to be the "ur" of the word future, *futūrus (futūra, futūrum)* being none other than the future participle of the verb "to be" (*sum, esse*).

The future participle in Latin is used much as "about to" is in English: *Ursus imperātūrus est cerevisiam* (The bear is about to order a beer), *Animālia turturem ēssūra sunt* (The animals are about to eat the turtle), and so on.

The gerundive, sometimes known as the future passive participle, is formed by taking the nominative singular form of the present participle, removing its final *s* and adding *d* plus the endings for adjectives of the *bonus, bona, bonum* variety. Thus, *salūtandus, salūtanda, salūtandum*, worthy to be greeted, as in *Ursus cōmissimē salūtandus est* (The bear is to be greeted as politely as possible, The bear should be greeted as politely as possible, It is necessary that the bear be greeted as politely as possible, The bear has yet to be greeted as politely as possible, and so on).

The only tense of the indicative that we have not yet met is the future perfect, which is made by taking the stem of the perfect (the third principal part less the final -ī) and adding the endings -erō, -eris, -erit, -erimus, -eritis, -erint. All but the last of these endings look suspiciously like the future forms of the verb *sum, esse*, which they probably are. Thus: *dīxerō, dīxeris, dīxerit, dīxerimus, dīxeritis, dīxerint* (I will have said, you will have said, and so forth).

Vocabulary

ēvānescō, ēvānescere, ēvānui,
——to vanish
edō, edere (ēsse), ēdī, ēssum (ēsum) to eat; this verb has the pieces of two different conjugations in its bag of tricks. The present active indicative is: *edō, ēs (edis), ēst (edit), edimus, ēstis (editis), edunt*; you make (or recognize) the other forms by treating *edō, edere, ēdī, ēssum* as though it were a regular *-ere* verb (remember about *d* plus *t* winding up as *s*), except maybe for the long vowel in the fourth principal part, but it's only fair to say that lots of fourth principal parts have long vowels where they

might have been expected to have short ones. (This little-understood phenomenon is the ostensible result of something called Lachmann's Rule, Lachmann's because someone named Lachmann thought it up, and Rule—as opposed to Law—because nobody really believes it.) If you run across any forms that look as though they belonged to *sum, esse* but have a long *e*, they go here.
vertō, vertere, vertī, versum to turn (around), to change; cf. *versus* against; and *recto* (the regular, correct, right side) vs. *verso* (the flip side)
fungus, fungī (m.) mushroom

84

rārō seldom, rarely

petasus, petasī (m.) hat

autem on the other hand, moreover, however

exspectō, exspectāre, exspectāvī, exspectātum (sometimes just plain *exp-*) to await

mē reditūrum i.e., me who is about to return

hiems, hiemis (f.) winter, stormy, cold season

aestās, aestātis (f.) summer

Via Appia, Viae Appiae (f.) Appian Way, a road that ran from Rome down the coast through Naples to Brindisi, begun by one Appius Claudius Caecus

proximō diē on the next day

saltō, saltāre, saltāvī, —— to dance, jump

lūna, lūnae (f.) moon

caniculus, caniculī (m.) little dog; *-ulus, -ula, -ulum* is a popular Latin diminutive suffix

rīdeō, rīdēre, rīsī, rīsum to laugh

lūcerna, lūcernae (f.) lamp; cf. *lūx, lūcis* (f.) light and

lūcifer, lūcifera, lūciferum light-bearer, light-bringer

pendō, pendere, pependī, pēnsum to cause to hang, to hang

fenestra, fenestrae (f.) window

Alba Longa, Albae Longae (f.) The city, as legend has it, where Romulus and Remus were born; hence the mother of Rome.

peregrīnus, peregrīnī (m.) foreigner, pilgrim

vestiō, vestīre, vestīvī, vestītum to clothe, dress

etrūscus, etrūsca, etrūscum Etruscan

dūcō, dūcere, dūxī, ductum to lead

crapšti the epithet *crapšti* is never fully explained

explicō, explicāre, explicāvī, explicātum to unfold, explain; cf. *plicō, plicāre, plicāvī, plicātum* to fold

omnis, omne (gen. *omnis*) all, every; pl. everybody

mendāx, mendācis (m.) liar

vēritās, vēritātis (f.) truth; cf. *vērō* truly, in truth

I. Translate into English

a. *Factūrus sum iter ad Morbōniam in nāve, ut iter faciendum est. Iter ita faciendum est quia Morbōnia in īnsulā est.*

b. *Petasus meus triquetrus;*
   Triquetrus petasus meus.
   Sī nōn esset triquetrus,
   Nōn esset ēssendus.

c. *Exībō etiam; tū autem hīc manēbis ut exspectēs mē reditūrum.*

d. *Calceōs nostrōs hieme edere poterimus calceīs vestrīs in aestāte ēssīs.*

e. *Sī nocte pervēnerimus, Viā Appiā ierimus; sī proximō diē viā dē Morbōnia.*

II. Translate into Latin

a. If my hat didn't have three corners (if my hat weren't three-cornered), it would be grandpa.

b. If a man will ask a man "Are you a bear, or are you a man?" the other will rarely say "I am a bear."

c. If the cow is not able to jump over the moon, the little dog will not be able to laugh seeing the cow jumping over the moon.

d. If the soldiers are going to come by the Appian Way, one lamp is to be hung in the window of the tower.

e. If, however, they are going to come by the road from Morbonia, a plucked chicken is to be thrown over the wall of the university.

III. *Fābula: "Ubi Alba Longa?"*

Peregrīnus Rōmā ad Albam Longam iter faciēbat. Ad trivium

pervēnit ubi sedentēs duōs hominēs vīdit vestītōs modō Etrūscōrum. Ambōbus salūtātis, rogāvit peregrīnus: "Via ad dexteramne dūcet ad Albam Longam?" Dīxit ūnus: "Crapšti."

Explicāvit alter rīdēns: "Amīcus meus dīxit 'Sīc,' sed, ut omnēs in terrā etrūscā, mendāx est."

Scienda est aut necne peregrīnō vēritās?

CHAPTER IX

Demonstrative Pronouns:
This, That, and the Others

Caesar tells us in the opening line of *Dē Bellō Gallicō* that Gaul was a totality which was divided into three parts (*Gallia est omnis dīvīsa in partēs trēs*). This useful piece of information was undoubtedly placed at the very beginning of the book because the author was, if nothing else, a clever strategist: catch the reader's eye with a good opener, and you've got him. And if there was anything dearer to a Roman's heart and mind than the number two, it was surely the number three. It's a safe bet in any case that if Caesar had started his book, "Gaul is a totality which is divided into several parts, I don't know, say, seventeen or eighteen or so," it would never have received the widespread critical acclaim that it has over the millennia since its first edition.

In any event, three was, as numbers went, a heavy one for speakers of Latin in general, and in particular for the legions of the Roman army, which carried the Latin language into Gaul. For a legion (*legiō, legiōnis*) was itself a totality which was divided into three parts: the infantry, or foot soldiers (*peditēs, peditum*), the cavalry, or horse soldiers (*equitēs, equitum*), and the auxiliary troops, or help soldiers (*auxilia, auxiliōrum*). The last included specialists in such popular instruments of destruction as the catapult (*catapulta, catapultae*), the sling (*funda, fundae*), and the arrow (*sagitta, sagittae*). Foot soldiers largely made do with the lance (*pīlum, pīlī*) and the double-edged sword (*gladius, gladiī*). Interestingly enough, the bulk of the cavalry and *auxilia* was, by Caesar's time, made up of non-Romans, people who had in fact been conquered by the Romans. The infantry was probably in it for the money, which gives you an idea of the sort of Latin that the army took with it on its travels.

Originally, the army had been made up of land-holding citizens (as opposed to just anybody, like slaves and the poor). But that was in the days when the army was essentially a defensive organization. When the powers that were got around to taking the offensive, army life rapidly lost its appeal, and the requirement that catapult fodder had to be well-to-do was quietly swept under the rug, though, technically, you still had to be a citizen to get out there and fight.

So the army, like Gaul, was a collection of these guys, those guys, and the other guys. The way you distinguish among them from the safety of your armchair is with the following pronouns, called demonstratives because they point out (show) which is which. The first means "this, this one, this-here (these, these ones, these-here)."

SINGULAR

	MASC	FEM	NEUT
NOM	hic	haec	hoc
GEN	huius	huius	huius
DAT	huic	huic	huic
ACC	hunc	hanc	hoc
ABL	hōc	hāc	hōc

PLURAL

	MASC	FEM	NEUT
NOM	hī	hae	haec
GEN	hōrum	hārum	hōrum
DAT	hīs	hīs	hīs
ACC	hōs	hās	haec
ABL	hīs	hīs	hīs

With "this" may be contrasted two kinds of "that." *Ille, illa, illud* means "that, that one, that-there (those, those ones, those-there)." *Iste, ista, istud* originally meant "that near you, that one over by you," but it later came to have a pejorative flavor to it, at about which time the army took it far and wide, soldiers' vocabulary being no more genteel then than it is now.

SINGULAR

	MASC		FEM		NEUT	
NOM	ille	iste	illa	ista	illud	istud
GEN	illīus	istīus	illīus	istīus	illīus	istīus
DAT	illī	istī	illī	istī	illī	istī
ACC	illum	istum	illam	istam	illud	istud
ABL	illō	istō	illā	istā	illō	istō

PLURAL

	MASC		FEM		NEUT	
NOM	illī	istī	illae	istae	illa	ista
GEN	illōrum	istōrum	illārum	istārum	illōrum	istōrum
DAT	illīs	istīs	illīs	istīs	illīs	istīs
ACC	illōs	istōs	illās	istās	illa	ista
ABL	illīs	istīs	illīs	istīs	illīs	istīs

Alius, alia, aliud (other) is declined like these "thats," except that, of course, the masculine nominative singular form, *alius*, ends in *-us* and not *-e*.

Finally, it wouldn't be Latin if there weren't a demonstrative that is neither "this" nor "that," but a neutral combination of the two (this, that, he, she, it). Such is *is, ea, id*:

SINGULAR

	MASC	FEM	NEUT
NOM	is	ea	id
GEN	eius	eius	eius
DAT	eī	eī	eī
ACC	eum	eam	id
ABL	eō	eā	eō

PLURAL

	MASC	FEM	NEUT
NOM	eī	eae	ea
GEN	eōrum	eārum	eōrum
DAT	eīs	eīs	eīs
ACC	eōs	eās	ea
ABL	eīs	eīs	eīs

And as *is, ea, id* goes, so goes "the same" (*īdem, eadem, idem*):

SINGULAR

	MASC	FEM	NEUT
NOM	īdem	eadem	idem
GEN	eiusdem	eiusdem	eiusdem
DAT	eīdem	eīdem	eīdem
ACC	eundem	eandem	idem
ABL	eōdem	eādem	eōdem

PLURAL

	MASC	FEM	NEUT
NOM	eīdem	eaedem	eadem
GEN	eōrundem	eārundem	eōrundem
DAT	eisdem	eisdem	eisdem
ACC	eōsdem	eāsdem	eadem
ABL	eisdem	eisdem	eisdem

Vocabulary

gallicus, gallica, gallicum Gallic

pars, partis (f.) part, portion

legiō, legiōnis (f.) legion; a legion was as large a unit as there was (short of army, or maybe two legions) in the Roman army. Typically, an *imperātor* (gen. *imperātōris*) or general (the guy who gives the orders) commanded two or more legions. A legion was composed of ten *cohortēs*, a *cohors* being a company of three *manipulī*, a *manipulus* being a division of two *centuriae*, a *centuria* being, as the name implies, a company of one hundred men.

pedes, peditis (m.) foot soldier, infantryman

eques, equitis (m.) horseman, member of the cavalry; cf. *equus, equī* (m.) horse

auxilium, auxiliī (n.) aid, help; *auxilia, auxiliōrum* helps, i.e., extra help

catapulta, catapultae (f.) catapult

funda, fundae (f.) sling

sagitta, sagittae (f.) arrow

pīlum, pīlī (n.) lance

gladius, gladiī (m.) sword

hic, haec, hoc this, this one

ille, illa, illud that, that one

iste, ista, istud that near you, that one by you

alius, alia, aliud other

is, ea, id this, that, he, she, it

īdem, eadem, idem same

Caesar, Caesaris (m.) Caesar

fossa, fossae (f.) ditch, trench; a Roman camp (*castra, castrōrum*, literally, forts) typically consisted of a square area surrounded by a trench (*fossa*) beyond which was a rampart (*agger, aggeris*) made of the dirt that formerly lived in the *fossa*. On top of the *agger* was constructed a stockade called a *vallum*, so called because it was made of *vallī* (pikes).

fodiō, fodere, fōdī, fossum to dig

centuriō, centuriōnis (m.) centurion, commander of a *centuria*; the chief centurion was called a *prīmipīlus*. Above him in rank were the *tribūnī militum* of which there were six per legion. Above the *tribūnī* was the *lēgātus* (literally, delegate),

centurio, continued
and above him, the *quaestor.*
A *quaestor* was originally a
provincial governor's chief
of staff in charge of financial
affairs. (Caesar was sent to
Spain as *quaestor* early in
his career to straighten out
that province's finances.)
But the luckier *quaestores*
got to lead troops into
battle. Above the *quaestor*
was the *praetor.*

dum while

facillime most easily; cf. *facilis,
facile* (gen. *facilis*) easy

pugnus, pugni (m.) fist; *pug-*

num facere to make a fist

pro before, in front of, for
(with the ablative)

fortis, forte (gen. *fortis*) strong;
fortissime most strongly, as
strongly as possible

ferio, ferire, —, —, to hit,
smite

*removeo, removere, removi,
remotum* to remove, move
back, withdraw

dolor, doloris (m.) pain,
anguish

nunc now

intellegens (gen. *intellegentis*)
intelligent, smart

I. Translate into English

   a. *In hac taberna imperavit cerevisiam Caesar; in illa, Pythagoras.*
   b. *O si legiones eius Morboniam abissent!*
   c. *Pedes stultus in ista catapulta erat.*
   d. *Nonnulli equites in hos agros gallicos ierunt; alii autem in
      pomarium cucurrerunt.*
   e. *Turture legato, cervus hunc manipulum imperabit; tu, o lupe,
      istum.*

II. Translate into Latin

   a. If you've seen this turtle (this turtle having been seen), you've
      seen them all.
   b. It's the same bear in a different story.

c. These two bears are not the same bears, but they *are* brothers.

d. That other bear is not their brother but their mother.

e. The Gallic legions are in that ditch; those of yours are in an apple tree.

III. *Fābula*

Duo peditēs legiōnis Caesaris fossam fodiēbant. Dīxit ūnus alterō, "Nōnne vidēs centuriōnem super aggerem castrōrum? Mē rogābam: 'Quārē super aggerem stat ille, dum nōs in hāc fossā fodimus?' " Respondit eī alter, "Hoc nōn sciō. Ut rogēs eum."

Pedes ad centuriōnem vēnit et rogāvit eum, "Quārē super aggerem stās dum nōs in illā fossā fodimus?" Respondit eī centuriō, "Hoc facillimē dēmonstrandum est." Centuriō pugnum fēcit prō vallō, dīcēns peditī, "Pugnum meum fortissimē ferī." Pedes pugnum centuriōnis ferītūrus erat cum alter celerrimē pugnum removit. Pedes ergō fortissimē vallum ferīvit. Dolor! Dīxit centuriō, "Nunc scīsne quārē stō ego super aggerem dum vōs in illā fossā foditis? Ego intellegēns, vōs stultī." "Sīc," respondit pedes, et rediit in fossam.

Amīcus eius rogāvit eum, "Centuriō dīxitne tibi quārē super aggerem stat ille dum nōs in fossā fodimus?" "Vērō," respondit eī alter. "Facillimē est dēmonstrandum." Et pugnum faciēns prō ōre dīxit amīcō, "Pugnum meum fortissimē ferī."

CHAPTER X

Leading Questions, Complex Sentences or, Before the Law

Roman law and the administration of Roman justice was not always (if ever) all that it has subsequently been cracked up to have been. Before 450 B.C., the custodians of the law were the ruling nobles, the *patriciī*. These worthies took their job very seriously and so conspired to keep the average Joe, or *plēbs*, from finding out just what the law was. Since (perhaps not altogether surprisingly) the average Joe was the one who almost invariably seemed to wind up being the defendant, the *plēbēs* soon began to ask such questions as "What is the law?" (*"Quid est lēx?"*), "Who'll keep an eye on the keepers of the law?" (*"Quis custōdiet lēgis custōdēs?"*), and "Who's the law for anyway?" (*"Quibus etiam est lēx?"*).

These questions represented a major breakthrough, for it was now clear that the *plēbēs* had gotten their hands on the interrogative pronoun ("who?", "what?"), which is declined as follows:

SINGULAR

	MASC	FEM	NEUT
NOM	quis	quis	quid
GEN	cuius	cuius	cuius
DAT	cui	cui	cui
ACC	quem	quem	quid
ABL	quō	quō	quō

PLURAL

	MASC	FEM	NEUT
NOM	quī	quae	quae
GEN	quōrum	quārum	quōrum
DAT	quibus	quibus	quibus
ACC	quōs	quās	quae
ABL	quibus	quibus	quibus

It also meant that the *plēbēs* were not going to put up with this situation too much longer. The nobles hastily suggested that a committee be set up to study the matter, and in short order the law was written down for all to see and understand (assuming that everybody could read; by and large, of course, they couldn't). The laws were written down on twelve bronze tablets and placed in the center of town. Actually, the process took two steps. First, the laws were written down on *ten* bronze tablets and placed in the center of town. Later, two tablets of supplementary laws were added to take care of some things that had slipped everybody's mind earlier but which, fortunately, had been spotted in the nick of time by one sharp-witted ruler or another.

The law applied to Roman citizens. While the Roman Empire consisted of only the city of Rome, this restriction inconvenienced only slaves, children, and, to an extent, women. When Rome began to expand, gobbling up widely flung territories inhabited by people who already had their own laws, the plan was that local law would apply but would be administered by the Rome-appointed governor. This eventually gave way to a new and improved system, from the Romans' point of view, at least: citizenship for virtually everybody.

But, down to brass (or bronze) tacks, the actual comeuppancing of wrongdoers. First, you have to ask "Who dunnit?" (*"Quis fēcit istud?"*) and "What did he (she) do?" (*"Quid fēcit ille (illa)?"*), using, in so doing, the interrogative pronouns just presented. With any luck, the culprit will step forward, saying, "It's my fault!" (*"Mea culpa!"*) or, more likely, "Behold the wrongdoer: that guy!" (*"Ecce malefactor: ille!"*)

There are more elegant possibilities. For example, "Behold the evildoer who did the evil deed!" (*"Ecce malefactor quī maleficium commīsit!"*) or "Behold the evildoer whom ye seek!" (*"Ecce malefactor quem quaeritis!"*), for which at least a passing acquaintance with the relative pronouns is required.

The relative pronouns are those "whos," "whoms," "whats," "whiches," and "thats" that show up in statements like "I know *who* did it," "I know to *whom* it was done," "I know *what* he did," "The evil deed, *which* I saw, was done by George," and "The evil *that* men do is not to be known." They may be contrasted with their close cousins, the interrogative pronouns, which show up in questions, like *"Who* did it?" *"What* did the culprit do?" "To *whom* did he do it?" While in English, these "cousins" are so close as to require a chromosome count to distinguish the one from the other; in Latin, they speak, if not for themselves, for whom?

SINGULAR

	MASC	FEM	NEUT
NOM	qui	quae	quod
GEN	cuius	cuius	cuius
DAT	cui	cui	cui
ACC	quem	quam	quod
ABL	quō	quā	quō

PLURAL

	MASC	FEM	NEUT
NOM	qui	quae	quae
GEN	quōrum	quārum	quōrum
DAT	quibus	quibus	quibus
ACC	quōs	quās	quae
ABL	quibus	quibus	quibus

You cannot neglect the nominative, accusative, and ablative singular. But if you've troubled to learn the interrogative pronouns (already?), you are home free, which is more than Roman slaves, children, and women were.

For the culprit whose grasp of Latin is tenuous, there are other no less elegant things that can be said when stepping forward to accuse the just fellow of the misdeed. For example, *"Sciō illum malefactōrem esse"* ("I know that he's the evildoer," literally, "I know him to be the evildoer"). This is called indirect statement and is a favorite Latin construction. It starts off with the subject knowing, perceiving, thinking, or just plain saying that somebody (in the accusative) did something. The doing something is expressed in this kind of sentence with an infinitive (or, sometimes, with a participle plus an infinitive).

Latin has three kinds of infinitive: present active, present passive, and perfect active. The present active infinitive is the one that ends in -*re*, as in *salūtāre* (to greet), *dīcere* (to say), and the like. (The corresponding passives "to be greeted," "to be said," and the like will be considered in Chapter XII.) The present infinitives are used in indirect statement when the action being known, perceived, thought, or said is roughly contemporaneous with the knowing, perceiving, thinking, or saying in question. Thus: *Putō illum adulterum esse* (I think that he's an adulterer), in which the thinking and the being are both going on now; *Dīxī illum adulterum esse* (I said that he was an adulterer), in which the saying and the being are both past; and *Dīcēs illum adulterum esse* (You will say that he is an adulterer), in which everything is in the murky future.

The perfect active infinitive is formed by taking the perfect stem and adding -*isse*, as in *salūtāvisse* (to have greeted) and *dīxisse* (to have said). This is used in indirect statement when the action being reported is prior to the reporting. Thus: *Putō illum adulterum fuisse* (I know that he was an adulterer); *Dīxī illum adulterum fuisse* (I said that he had been an adulterer); and *Dīcēs illum adulterum fuisse* (You will say that he was an adulterer).

Indirect statement in which the reported action is to take place (or is to have taken place) after the time of the report uses the future participle plus the infinitive *esse* (to be). Thus: *Putō illum adulterum futūrum esse* (I know that he's going to be an adulterer); *Dīxī illum adulterum futūrum esse* (I said that he was going to be an adulterer); and *Dīcēs illum adulterum futūrum esse* (You will say that he's going to be an adulterer).

Incidentally, in case you were wondering whether Latin is ambiguous, as is English, when it comes to such statements as "He knows that he did it" and "She said she'd do it" (where there's some question as to how many different people are actually involved), the answer is no. (Obviously, the problem only arises in the third person, since there's only one "me" and only one "you" or

100

"youse" on any given occasion.) To handle such cases, Latin has a set of reflexive pronouns, that is, pronouns that are used when the subject of a sentence is seen lurking about elsewhere in the sentence: "She said that she (herself) would do it," "He ordered a beer for himself (but nothing for me)," and the like. The third person reflexive pronoun goes as follows:

	SINGULAR	PLURAL
NOM	——	——
GEN	suī	suī
DAT	sibi	sibi
ACC	sē (or sēsē)	sē (or sēsē)
ABL	sē (or sēsē)	sē (or sēsē)

The possessive pronoun that goes with "himself, herself, itself, themselves" is *suus, sua, suum*. Thus: *Dīxit sē adulterum esse* (He said he was an adulterer, that is, he said that he himself was an adulterer), with which may be contrasted *Dīxit eum adulterum esse* (He said that he was an adulterer, that is, he said that somebody else was an adulterer). Likewise, *Dīcunt sē adulterōs nōn esse* (They say that they themselves aren't adulterers), with which may be contrasted *Dīcunt illōs adulterōs nōn esse* (They say that those guys aren't adulterers).

Let us briefly return to our culprit, or to someone like him, for two final observations. The culprit may say, as he quietly disappears, "Whoever did this is certainly a bad guy" (*"Quis fēcit istud malefactor est vērō"*), for which something called indefinite pronouns is or are necessary, the words that mean "whoever, whatever, whomever, someone, anyone," and so on. Indefinite pronouns in Latin, fortunately, look exactly like the interrogatives, and you know they are not interrogatives because there's no question mark at the end of the sentence. (Actually, that's not quite right, if you're splitting hairs, though "Would anyone (someone) like a beer?" is really the same as "Who (if anyone) would like a beer?") The indefinites (*quis, quid*) are routinely confused with "he who" and "she who" who, when in Rome, go under the name of *quī, quae, quod.* Thus: *Quī fēcērunt ista malefactōrēs sunt* (Whoever did these things are bad guys, or, Those who did these things are bad guys).

Alternatively, the culprit may ask, *"Mihi licetne advocātum advocāre?"* ("May I call a lawyer?")

Vocabulary

patricius, patriciī (m.) patrician, noble; cf. *patria, patriae* (f.) fatherland, country

plēbs, plēbis (f.) plebeian, commoner

quis, quid who?, what? (interrogative pronoun)

lēx, lēgis (f.) law; *lēx duodecim tabulārum* the law of the Twelve Tables

custōs, custōdis (m., f.) guard, keeper; cf. *custōdiō, custōdīre, custōdīvī, custōdītum* to guard, keep watch

culpa, culpae (f.) guilt, fault

malefactor, malefactōris (m.) evildoer

quī, quae, quod who, which (relative pronoun)

putō, putāre, putāvī, putātum to think

suī, etc. himself, herself, itself, themselves (third person reflexive pronoun)

suus, sua, suum his, her, its, their (reflexive: in "He ate his lunch," if it was his own lunch, it would be *suus*; if someone else's, *eius*, the genitive of *is, ea, id*). Third persons are often hard to tell apart. A useful aid is the demonstrative pronoun *ipse, ipsa, ipsum* (self, that very) which is declined like *ūnus, ūna, ūnum.*

quis, quid whoever, whatever, somebody, something (indefinite pronoun); cf. *tertium quid* a third something or whatsis

qui, quae, quod he who, she who, etc. This is really no more than a slightly elliptical use of these guys in their regular hats, namely, as relative pronouns: the "he" or "she" or whatever has merely fallen by the wayside.

licet, licēre, licuit, ——(only in the third person singular and infinitive) to be allowed, permitted (with the dative): *mihi licet* I am allowed, *hominibus licet* men are allowed, and so on.

advocō, advocāre, advocāvī, advocātum to summon, call (especially to one's aid); *advocātus, advocātī* (m.) someone summoned (to aid you), specifically, a lawyer; cf. also *vōx, vōcis* (f.) voice

nōlō, nōlle, nōluī, ——to not wish, to not want; the imperatives *nōlī* and *nōlīte* are often used to tell somebody not to do something (You don't want to do that, do you). *Nōlō* and company are perhaps best approached through *volō, velle, voluī,* ——to wish, want, which is conjugated as follows: present active indicative *volō,*

vīs, vult, volumus, vultis, volunt; imperfect active indicative *volēbam, volēbās,* etc.; future active *volam, volēs, volet, volēmus, volētis, volent*; the perfect and pluperfect active indicative and future perfect active are perfectly regular, as are the imperfect, perfect, and pluperfect active subjunctive. The present active subjunctive is: *velim, velīs, velit, velīmus, velītis, velint. Nōlō* is conjugated just like *volō* except that where *volō* has *vol-, nōlō* has *nōl-,* the one exception being the present active indicative: *nōlō, nōn vīs, nōn vult, nōlumus, nōn vultis, nōlunt.* Actually, it's only half an exception, as you can see.

aes, aeris (n.) copper, bronze; something made of copper or bronze, e.g., a bell

scrībō, scrībere, scrīpsī, scrīptum to write

nēmō nobody is declined thus: *nēmō, nūllīus, nēminī, nēminem, nūllō* (m., n.) and *nūllā* (f.). The plural of *nūllus, nūlla, nūllum* is used for more than one nobody at a time.

nihil (indeclinable) nothing cf.
  nihilum, nihilī (n.), which
  also signifies "nothing"
petasātus, petasāta, petasātum
  wearing a hat, behatted
pōnō, pōnere, posuī, positum
  to put, place
clāvus, clāvī (m.) nail, peg
caput, capitis (n.) head
praetor, praetōris (m.) magistrate. In precolonial days,
  the *praetor* was the man in
  charge of administering
  justice. As Rome expanded,
  there got to be two varieties
  of *praetor*, the *praetor*
  urbānus, who took care of
  cases involving Roman citizens, and the *praetor pere-*
  grīnus, who handled disputes
  among foreigners.
tenebricōsus, tenebricōsa,
  tenebricōsum dark; cf.

tenebrae, tenebrārum darkness, shadows
niger, nigra, nigrum black
albus, alba, album white;
  petasī . . . vel nigrī vel albī
  the hats are black or white,
  i.e., some may be black and
  some may be white, or they
  may all be black or white
fax, facis (f.) torch
prīmus, prīma, prīmum first
color, colōris (m.) color
discō, discere, didicī, ——to
  learn, figure out
secundus, secunda, secundum
  second
perpetuitās, perpetuitātis (f.)
  perpetuity; *ad perpetuitā-*
  tem forever
lātum fourth principle part of
  ferō, ferre, tulī, lātum to
  carry, bring
dēnique at last
euhoe! hooray!

I. Translate into English.

   a. *Nōlī rogāre quid faciat tibi patria tua, sed cui resonet aes.*
   b. *Dīxērunt sē Etrūscōs esse, sed mendācēs vērō sunt.*
   c. *"Quod scrīpsī, scrīpsī"* (Pilate).
   d. *Sī quis roget "Quis est iste?" respondē "Nēmō;" sī "Quid*
  facit?" "Nihil."

e. *Introiēns petasātus eram*
   Petasum posuī in clāvō;
   Exiēns aut petasātus erō
   Aut caput cuius feriam.

II. Translate into Latin.

   a. He said that it was his own fault, but it wasn't.
   b. If anybody should think that you had spoken ill of me, he can
      (let him) go to hell.
   c. They said that whatever would be would be, but it wasn't.
   d. A man is allowed to call a lawyer; a wolf is allowed to call a
      snake.
   e. In which cask is the beer to be put?

III. *Fābula*

*Tribus malefactōribus dīxit praetor, "In spēluncam tenebricōsam
vōs dūcam. In spēluncā (in quā nihil videndum est propter tenebrās),
in capitibus vestrīs petasōs pōnam. Petasī quōs in capitibus vestrīs
pōnam vel nigrī vel albī erunt. Petasīs in capitibus positīs, ego exībō.
Redībō facem ferēns. Sī quis petasum nigrum videat, pugnum prō
ōre faciat. Illō quī prīmus colōrem petasī suī discat licēbit exīre:
līber erit. Secundō tertiōque autem exīre nōn licēbit: illī in spēluncā
manēbunt ad perpetuitātem."*

*Ita fuit. Face lātā, trēs ūnā pugnōs prō ōre fēcērunt. Nēmō autem
exiit, quia nēmō colōrem petasī suī didicit. Dēnique ūnus ex eīs ad
portam spēluncae cucurrit "Euhoe! Euhoe!" exclāmāns. Quis est
color petasī istīus?*

CHAPTER XI

Mūtātīs Mūtandīs
or,
The Expanding Woodwork

Sooner or later, generally sooner, the student of Latin angrily discovers that Latin involves learning one hell of a lot of grammar. Traditional responses to this lamentation have tended to range from "If you can't stand the heat, stay out of the kitchen" to "What if your face froze like that?"

With the advent of modern linguistic theory, two further responses have made their appearance: "All languages, on close inspection, turn out to be of equal complexity, so Latin is no worse than any other"; and "Languages tend to change, over time, in the direction of greater simplicity, so be thankful that you don't have to learn Proto-Indo-European." (The third thinkable view of linguistic entropy—that languages tend to change, over time, in the direction of greater complexity—has been thought to be about as congruent as the notion that the longer the system runs, the less energy is required to keep it rolling.)

One thing is fairly certain: Latin has done away with a number of horrors that you would have to learn if you were studying Proto-Indo-European. We have already tendered our respects (in Chapter III) on the sad passing of the dual. Proto-Indo-European clearly distinguished among the singular, dual, and plural in nouns, adjectives, and verbs. Eventually, the Latini and practically everybody else said, "Enough is enough, and dual is plural," throwing out the old dual endings—keeping only a few souvenirs, like the declension of "two" and "both"—and swelling the ranks of the plurals. This is the usual linguistic scenario: keep one or two traces of the original and throw the rest in with the never more logical grammar that ultimately prevails. This makes the traces irregular where they used to be quite regular. *Sīc friat crustulum* (Thus crumbleth the little cake).

Other instances of this process of regularizing are legion. Proto-Indo-European seems to have had a "perfect" and an "aorist" in its verbal system that have been lumped together in the Latin perfect, which is regular to the extent of having one set of endings and, for some kinds of verbs, a rule of thumb that tells you how to get the stem from something else that you presumably already know. The imperative mood offers a similar, somewhat watered-down example of this apparent grammatical must. We've already encountered "Hey, do it yourself" and "Hey, do it yourselves" in Latin. Proto-Indo-European undoubtedly had, in addition to these, third person imperatives, like "Hey, he should do it himself," "Hey, let him do it himself," "Hey, they should do it themselves," "Hey, let them do it themselves." These are found in older Latin, Greek, and their grizzled contemporaries, but generally get replaced by the subjunctive later. If PIE had a set of first person imperatives—"I should do it myself," "We should do it ourselves"—these have been shunted off into the subjunctive or, in the languages fortunate enough to have preserved it, the optative; or both. (The less said about the optative, the better.)

The way, incidentally, that older Latin made the third person imperatives, "let him" and "let them," was as follows. First of all, they called them "future imperatives" and had a pair of second person forms to go with them. The way you made the second and third person singular (which were identical in form) was to take the third person present active indicative form of the verb and add *-ō*. In the case of *-āre, -ēre,* and *-īre* verbs, you also had to lengthen the theme vowel: *Cerevisiam imperātō!* (Thou shalt order a beer! Let him order a beer!), *Hīc manētō!* (You will stay here! Let him stay here!), *Mihi audītō!* (You'd better listen to me! He'd better listen to me!) as against *Ursum capitō!* (You must seize the bear! He must seize the bear!) and *Ursō dīcitō "Vālē!"* (Say "good-bye" to the bear! He must say "good-bye" to the bear!). To make the second person plural, you merely add *-te* to the second person singular: *Cerevisiam imperātōte!* (You-all will have to order the beer!), and the like. The third person plural takes the form of the third person plural present active indicative and adds *-ō* to it, with no commotion: thus *Cerevisiam recipiuntō, cerevisiam amantō!* (They'll get beer and like it!)

The Romans also made cuts in both the number of cases and the number of declensions, i.e., sets of case endings. Proto-Indo-European seems to have had, besides nominative, vocative, genitive, dative, accusative, and ablative cases, an "instrumental" and a "locative" case as well. The instrumental case was used to say "by means of" what or which, a function that the Latin ablative has pretty much absorbed. The locative told you where. Again, the Latin ablative has taken this burden on as well, though there are traces of the original in spots. If you wanted to say "in Rome," "at Rome," for example, it was *Rōmae* (not the ablative *Rōmā*), which, of course, *looks* like a genitive, adding to the fun and con-

108

fusion. No wonder that people took to using *in* plus the ablative (or *apud*, at the place of, with, plus the accusative).

The consolidation of the declensions didn't happen without a fight either, or so we are told by the survivors, many of whom went to live out their final years in the relative peace and quiet of the third declension, from which such disparate mates as the *i* stems, consonant stems, and mixed *i* stems will be recalled from Chapter III if necessary. To these could be added the patriarchal *pater familiās* (father, head of the household) in which the *-ās* is an old genitive singular ending, otherwise lost and gone forever in all but early Latin.

Latin's ever-diminishing fourth declension has what's left of the Indo-European *u* stems:

SINGULAR

	MASC	FEM	NEUT
NOM	condus	manus	cornū
GEN	condūs	manūs	cornūs
DAT	conduī (condū)	manuī (manū)	cornū
ACC	condum	manum	cornū
ABL	condū	manū	cornū

PLURAL

	MASC	FEM	NEUT
NOM	condūs	manūs	cornua
GEN	conduum	manuum	cornuum
DAT	condibus	manibus	cornibus
ACC	condūs	manūs	cornua
ABL	condibus	manibus	cornibus

condus, condūs, shopkeeper; *manus, manūs* hand; *cornū, cornūs* horn.

What eventually happens to the fourth declension is previewed in the declension of *domus, domūs* (or *domī*), house:

SINGULAR		PLURAL
NOM	domus	domūs
GEN	domūs (domī)	domuum (domōrum)
DAT	domuī (domō)	domibus
ACC	domum	domūs (domōs)
ABL	domū (domō)	domibus

In short, nouns of the fourth declension quietly insinuate themselves into the second declension. (If there were ever any fourth declension adjectives, they had all hot-footed it into the second declension before they got to Latin.) *Domī*, by the way, is really a locative, like *Rōmae*, and is only used as such until *domus* becomes a full-time second declension noun.

Two things kept the ever-dwindling fourth declension alive. First, some words that got used enough so that they couldn't merge into another declension without being noticed and, second, the supine. The useful words include some of the parts of the body, such as hand (*manus*), knee (*genū*), and horn (*cornū*). The supine, which is found only in the accusative and dative or ablative – the dative in *-uī* – is a phonus bolonus from the second declension, and the *real* one ends in *-ū* like the ablative – and has managed to get the job of fourth principal part of the verb. The supine is essentially a noun made from a verb and can usually be translated as "for the purpose of verbing, to verb," as in *In tabernam introiit ursus cerevisiam imperātum* (The bear went into a bar for the purpose of ordering a beer) and the old standard, *Mīrābile dictū* (Marvelous to tell, i.e., Marvelous for telling you about).

Before you make up your mind about entropy, whether things stay essentially the same or whether they get easier or harder, the fifth declension should be introduced in evidence. The fifth declension has all of two full-time members, that is, two nouns for which all the case forms can be found in the writings of one Latin author or another. (There are a very few part-time members of the fifth declension as well.) Not very many, when you think of it, but neatness is the sign of an orderly mind, so what can you say? The two nouns which are attested in all their forms are *rēs* (thing), and *diēs* (day), which tells you something right there: the fifth declension is living off the proceeds of two *very* useful vocabulary items, which are declined as follows:

	SINGULAR		PLURAL	
NOM	rēs	diēs	rēs	diēs
GEN	reī	diēī (diē)	rērum	diērum
DAT	reī	diēī (diē)	rēbus	diēbus
ACC	rem	diem	rēs	diēs
ABL	rē	diē	rēbus	diēbus

The point is this: the fourth and fifth declensions, like the mixed *i* stems and the number 2, are ten *dēnāriī* apiece, but two for a *sēstertium*, which is how languages *really* change.

Vocabulary

mūtō, mūtāre, mūtāvī, mūtā-tum to change; *mūtātis mūtandis* the things to be changed having been changed

friō, friāre, ·——, —— to crumble

crustulum, crustulī (n.) little cake

apud with, at the house of, according to (with the accusative)

condus, condūs (m.) shopkeeper

manus, manūs (f.) hand

cornū, cornūs (n.) horn

domus, domūs (domī) (f.) house

genū, genūs (n.) knee

mīrābilis, mīrābile (gen. *mīrā-bilis*) marvelous

rēs, reī (f.) thing

diēs, diēī (diē) (m.) day

vēnātor, vēnātōris (m.) hunter
bōzō, bōzūs (m.) clown. Latin has borrowed, to nobody's surprise, a number of Greek nouns which it deferentially spells and declines funny. Pay it no mind.
ambulō, ambulāre, ambulāvī, ambulātum to go, walk
magnus, magna, magnum big, great
parvus, parva, parvum small
foedus, foeda, foedum ugly
appropinquō, appropinquāre, appropinquāvī, appropinquā-

-tum to approach, draw near
coram face to face, facing
crocodīlus, crocodīlī (m.) crocodile
ante before (with the accusative)
cauda, caudae (f.) tail
praecīdō, praecīdere, praecīdī, praecīsum to cut off
pingo, pingere, pinxī, pictum to paint; cf. *Pictī, Pictōrum* Picts, so called because they painted themselves blue and rode out naked against the Romans

I. Translate into English.

   a. *Sī essēs hic, domī essēs.*
   b. *Avis in manū cerevisia in manū nōn parēs.*
   c. *Vēnātor cornua in mūrō pōnit; adulterī, in capite vēnātōris.*
   d. *Pedes in fossā melior quam duōs ursōs in aggerō.*
   e. *Vēnērunt, facillimē dictū, ursum salūtātum, nōn cerevisiam imperātum.*

II. Translate into Latin

   a. These days are good, but those are noisome.
   b. We changed ourselves into horns.
   c. His horns are large but his mouth is small.
   d. We were all clowns in those matters (things).
   e. A clown on an island is worth three generals in Rome.

III. Fābula

Ambulābat homō cum cane magne suō in Viā Appiā. Alterum vīdit quī cum cane parvō foedōque appropinquābat. Prīmus sē dīxit, "Ille cum parvō cane suō in portam condūs ibant ut mihi liceat cum cane meō transīre." Sed ita nōn fuit. Hominēs (cum canibus suis) sē cōram ambulāvērunt. Caniculus foedus caput alterī ēdit. "?" exclāmāvit homō. "Rēs facillima dictū," dīxit homō quī cum caniculō foedō ambulāverat. "Canis meus crocodīlus erat ante caudam eius praecīsum et eum coloribus pīctum."

CHAPTER XII

Passives
and Passive-Aggressives

While it might have been possible for a Roman to be born, to live a full and rewarding life, and to die, never having learned about passives and deponents, it would certainly have been inconvenient at times and an utter conversation-stopper at others. Passives—I am being held prisoner, They were captured—are largely dispensable, because you can virtually always say the same thing with the appro-

114

priate active verbs—Somebody is holding me prisoner, Somebody captured them. It is probably for this reason that people eventually quit taking the trouble to learn them in Latin where, if you want to make a passive at somebody, you have to know a whole set of special verb endings.

Deponents, however, are another story. These are verbs which are conjugated as though they were passives but whose meaning is active. For example, compare the present indicatives.

SING	1.	adūror	hortor	videor	vereor
	2.	adūrāris	hortāris	vidēris	verēris
	3.	adūrātur	hortātur	vidētur	verētur
PLUR	1.	adūrāmur	hortāmur	vidēmur	verēmur
	2.	adūrāminī	hortāminī	vidēminī	verēminī
	3.	adūrantur	hortantur	videntur	verentur

Adūror I'm being burned, I am burned, *adūrārī* to be burned; *hortor* I'm urging, I urge, *hortārī* to urge; *videor* I'm being seen, I am seen, *vidērī* to be seen; *vereor* I'm afraid, I fear, *verērī* to be afraid.

SING	1.	dūcor	nāscor	sequor	capior
	2.	dūceris	nāsceris	sequeris	caperis
	3.	dūcitur	nāscitur	sequitur	capitur
PLUR	1.	dūcimur	nāscimur	sequimur	capimur
	2.	dūciminī	nāsciminī	sequiminī	capiminī
	3.	dūcuntur	nāscuntur	sequuntur	capiuntur

Dūcor I'm being led, I am led, *dūcī* to be led; *nāscor* I'm being born, I am born, *nāscī* to be born; *sequor* I'm following, I follow, *sequī* to follow; *capior* I'm being seized, I am seized, *capī* to be seized.

SING	1.	morior	audior	partior
	2.	moreris	audīris	partīris
	3.	moritur	audītur	partītur

	1.	morimur	audīmur	partīmur
PLUR	2.	morimini	audimini	partimini
	3.	moriuntur	audiuntur	partiuntur

Morior I'm dying, I die, *morī* to die; *audior* I'm being heard, I am heard, *audīrī* to be heard; *partior* I'm sharing, I share, *partīrī* to share.

The formation of passives and deponents is pretty straightforward, especially if you already know about actives. The present indicative, present subjunctive, imperfect indicative, imperfect subjunctive, and the future of passives can easily be made by taking the corresponding forms of the active, fiddling with them a little or not at all, and adding the endings *-r, -ris* (which sometimes shows up as *-re*), *-tur*, (or *-ur*, depending on how you count the *-t-*), *-mur, -mini* , and *-ntur* (or *-ur* again, depending on how you count the *-nt-*). The deponents are made in the same way except that you have to pretend that there's a set of active forms from which they may be derived, or just remember that they go like the passives and have done with it.

Taking *adūror, videor, dūcor, capior,* and *audior* as the passives that everything else is like, we might as well have a look at the present subjunctive, imperfect (indicative and subjunctive), and the future, leaving the other tenses until later.

You remember the imperfect active indicative from Chapter V: *adūrābam, vidēbam, dūcēbam, capiēbam, audiēbam; adūrābās, vidēbās, dūcēbās, capiēbās,* and so on. Well, the way you make the imperfect *passive* indicative is to take the first person singular form of the imperfect active indicative (*adūrābam, vidēbam,* and so on), remove the final *-m,* and add the personal endings of the passive, lengthening the *a* of the imperfect *-ba-* to *ā* in all persons but the first singular and third plural, sandwich fashion:

	1.	adūrābar	vidēbar	dūcēbar
SING	2.	adūrābāris	vidēbāris	dūcēbāris
	3.	adūrābātur	vidēbātur	dūcēbātur

116

	1.	adūrabāmur	vidēbāmur	dūcēbāmur
PLUR	2.	adūrabāminī	vidēbāminī	dūcēbāminī
	3.	adūrabantur	vidēbantur	dūcēbantur
				et cetera

The future passive works this way:

	1.	adūrābor	vidēbor	dūcar
SING	2.	adūrāberis	vidēberis	dūcēris
	3.	adūrābitur	vidēbitur	dūcētur
		etc.	etc.	etc.

As to the subjunctive, the present and imperfect are on much the same trip. The present subjunctive passive (cf. Chapter VII):

	1.	adūrer	videar	dūcar
SING	2.	adūrēris	videāris	dūcāris
	3.	adūrētur	videātur	dūcātur
		etc.	etc.	etc.

And the imperfect subjunctive passive (cf. Chapter VII):

	1.	adūrārer	vidērer	dūcerer
SING	2.	adūrārēris	vidērēris	dūcerēris
	3.	adūrārētur	vidērētur	dūcerētur
		etc.	etc.	etc.

You are no doubt still wondering about the deponents. They're called deponents because *dēpōnō, dēpōnere* means "to put aside, to put away" and Latin grammarians have generally observed that the significant thing about these verbs is that they've put their active forms in mothballs. What is not generally added is that, in their haste, the deponents have put aside the wrong set of meanings for those forms. The real story makes more sense.

Proto-Indo-European seems to have distinguished between two

117

"voices" in its verb system, the active and the middle. What apparently determined which got used on any occasion was the focus of the action of the verb: if the main interest in the sentence was the object of the subject's action, or the action itself, then the verb was active. If the focus was on the subject, however, the middle was used. Thus, "George hated his lunch" would have had an active verb, but both "George hated himself" and "George was hated" would have had middles. From middles in sentences like "George was hated" seem to have come the passives. The deponents in Latin tend to be verbs whose focus is always the subject and which, accordingly, would only have been conjugated in the middle voice in PIE: to be born, to die, to be afraid, and so on.

Vocabulary

adūrō, adūrāre, arūrāvī, adūrātum to burn

hortor, hortārī to urge, exhort

vereor, verērī to fear, be afraid

nāscor, nāscī to be born

sequor, sequī to follow

morior, morī to die. The past participle *mortuum* (dead) will be discussed in Chapter XIII.

partior, partīrī, to share

avetarda, avetardae (f.) bustard

dulcis, dulce (gen. *dulcis*) sweet, pleasant

decōrus, decōra, decōrum fit, seemly

amārus, amāra, amārum bitter

Vesuvius, Vesuviī (m.) Mount Vesuvius. This volcano was responsible, in its heyday, for the deaths of untold numbers of Latin speakers, including such notables as Pliny the Elder, who seems to have expired from inhaling too much sulfur dioxide during one of Vesuvius's more impressive public displays.

interficiō, interficere, interfēcī, interfectum to kill

nimis very much; *nimius* very very much

118

ōra, ōrae (f.) border, edge, region; *ōrae Acheruntis* (*Acherontis* in more modern dress) the underworld; cf. *ōrae lūminis* the upper world

īnfēlix, īnfēlicis (gen. *īnfēlicis*) unhappy

Orcus, Orcī (m.) one of the many lords of the underworld for speakers of Latin. Hell has always had rather fuzzy boundaries. For the Greeks, these were mostly aquatic, and the Romans splashed along with the game, at least officially. In practice, the Romans seem to have tolerated a variety of semiofficial beliefs about death and the thereafter. (Major controversies rage even now about what is to be or not to be inferred from the apparent coexistence of cremating and burying factions on the Italic peninsula.)

flūmen, flūminis (n.) river

rēgnum, rēgnī (n.) kingdom, realm; cf. *rēx, rēgis* (m.) king

dēsignō, dēsignāre, dēsignāvī, dēsignātum to name, designate

aspiciō, aspicere, aspēxī, aspectum to observe, behold, look at

multus, multa, multum many

corpus, corporis (n.) body

quatiō, quatere, quassī, quassum to shake

cēra, cērae (f.) wax

ferveō, fervēre, fervuī, —— to boil

conglaciō, conglaciāre, ——, —— to freeze

murmurō, murmurāre, murmurāvī, —— to murmur, mutter

stercus, stercoris (n.) dung, excrement

inquam, inquis, inquit, inquimus, inquiunt, . . . to say. This verb is "defective," i.e., only some of its forms are attested. Just as well, judging from the first person singular.

unda, undae (f.) wave

I. Translate into English

a. *"Avis, quae dīcitur 'avetarda,' bona est, sed putō hīc nōn habēre"* (Anthimus, *Dē Observātiōne Cibōrum*).

b. *Dulce et decōrum est prō patriā morī.*
c. *Amārum et indecōrum est ā Vesuviō interficī.*
d. *Quī nōn clāmant nōn audiuntur; quī autem nimius clāmant*
    nōn amantur.
e. *Iste capiātur quī in viam sē jactāvit.*

II. Translate into Latin

a. Let us follow those turtles into that bar.
b. Let them be led into the cave.
c. You were not being heard, o foot soldier, because you were in
    a trench.
d. Beer is ordered in a bar.
e. They will be caught by nobody.

III. *Fābula*

*Moritur malefactor et ad ōrās Acheruntis pervenit. Dīcit īnfēlīcī
Orcus, "Tria flūmina in rēgnō meō sunt. In ūnō ex eīs manēbis ad
perpetuitātem. Licet tibi autem flūmen dēsignāre in quō manēbis.
Venī ut flūmina aspiciās ante dēsignātum."*

*Orcum sequitur mortuus ad flūmina. In prīmō, multī videntur
quī clāmant, corpora quatientēs. "Nōlī in hoc flūmen introīre! Nōlī
introīre! Flūmen cēra fervēns!" In secundō, multī videntur quī
clāmant, corpora quatientēs. "Nōlī in hoc flūmen introīre! Nōlī
introīre! Flūmen nix conglaciāns frīgore!"*

*In tertiō, multī videntur quī murmurant, corpora minimē qua-
tientēs. "Quid est illud?" Orcum rogat malefactor. "Quid dīcunt
illī?" "Flūmen stercoris," inquit. "Dīcunt illī semper 'Nōlī undās
facere! Nōlī undās facere!' "*

CHAPTER XIII

The Long and the Short of It

Latin grammar books that fail to treat the subject of Latin meter and verse have always had a hard time securing the old *imprimātur* (or *imprimantur*). Or so we might infer from their relative scarcity. Even rarer are Latin grammar books that go to the bother of telling you all about the hard forms of the passives and deponents but then don't mention the easy ones, those of the perfect, pluperfect, and future perfect. This being the last chapter of the book, it is clearly now or never.

Passives and deponents may be dispatched quickly. All you have to know to be able to make the perfect, pluperfect, and future perfect of such verbs is (1) the past participle and (2) the present, imperfect, and future forms of the verb *sum* (to be). Two samples:

PERFECT INDICATIVE

SING	1.	adūrātus (adūrāta, adūrātum) sum	I was burned
	2.	adūrātus (adūrāta, adūrātum) es	you were burned
	3.	adūrātus (adūrāta, adūrātum) est	he (she, it) was burned
PLUR	1.	adūrāti (adūrātae, adūrāta) sumus	we were burned
	2.	adūrāti (adūrātae, adūrāta) estis	you were burned
	3.	adūrāti (adūrātae, adūrāta) sunt	they were burned
SING	1.	nātus (nāta, nātum) sum	I was born
	2.	nātus (nāta, nātum) es	you were born
	3.	nātus (nāta, nātum) est	he (she, it) was born
PLUR	1.	nātī (nātae, nāta) sumus	we were born
	2.	nātī (nātae, nāta) estis	you were born
	3.	nātī (nātae, nāta) sunt	they were born

Note that the past participle has to agree with the subject in both number and gender, and that the temptation to translate, e.g., *adūrātus sum* as "I *am* burned" instead of the more accurate "I *was* burned" is to be strenuously resisted.

As one might guess, the perfect subjunctive is made with the past participle and the present subjunctive forms of *sum* (*sim, sīs, sit,* etc.). Thus: *adūrātus (adūrāta, adūrātum) sim* (I may be burned), *nātus (nāta, nātum) sim* (I may be born), and the like. The pluperfect indicative is made with the past participle and the forms of the imperfect indicative of *sum*, e.g., *adūrātus (adūrāta, adūrātum) eram* (I had been burned), *nātus (nāta, nātum) eram* (I had been born). The corresponding subjunctive forms are used in making the pluperfect subjunctive: *adūrātus (adūrāta, adūrātum) essem, nātus (nāta, nātum) essem,* and so on. The future perfect (I will have been burned, born) is again the past participle plus the future of sum: *adūrātus (adūrāta, adūrātum) erō, nātus (nāta, nātum) erō,* and so on.

Some odds and ends: there are a very few verbs called semideponents, their claim to fame being that they are conjugated like active verbs in all tenses and moods except the five that we have just considered. Or, put another way, semideponents were off with the passives and deponents when the third principal parts were being handed out to the active verbs. *Fīdō, fīdere, fīsus sum* (to trust) is such a verb: *fīdō* (I trust), *fīdēbam* (I was trusting), *fīdam* (I will trust), but *fīsus sum* (I trusted), *fīsus eram* (I had trusted), and *fīsus erō* (I shall have trusted).

The present imperative of passives and deponents is made as follows: the second person singular looks to all intents and purposes to be the same as the active infinitive (or, for deponents, what the active infinitive would be if there were one). Thus, *Adūrāre!* (Be burned!), *Hortāre!* (Urge!), *Vidēre!* (Be seen!), *Verēre!* (Be afraid!), *Dūcere!* (Be led!), *Nāscere!* (Be born!), *Sequere!* (Follow!), *Capere!* (Be seized!), *Morere!* (Die!), *Audīre!* (Be heard!), *Partīre!* (Share!). The second person plural imperative is the same as the corresponding indicative: *Adūrāminī!* (Be ye burned!), and so on.

Now, then: about Latin verse, in which speakers of Latin have customarily said all that they had to say that they didn't prefer to say in prose. The earliest Latin verse form which has been identified is the Saturnian. That is, the Saturnian is the oldest verse form not obviously borrowed from the Greeks and in which, as it happens, the oldest surviving Latin poem is written, Livius Andronicus's (third century B.C.) translation of *The Odyssey*. If Latin speakers wrote poetry before this period, they didn't think to write it down and store it in a safe place, or, if they did, the place was so safe as to have eluded discovery for the past two thousand years.

It is not altogether clear how the Saturnian worked, that is, how it was supposed to be scanned. You might think that given a large enough sample, anybody who knew a little Latin (or less Greek) could easily see the pattern to it and could then tell you what was going on: there are so many syllables to a line or such and such a pattern of stressed and unstressed—or "long" and "short"—vowels. But no. The fact is that unless somebody gives you a copy of the

123

official rules beforehand, the scansion of poetry isn't always all that easy, especially if someone's put a Greek in your ear. (And do not be misled into thinking that it isn't still so, about having a Greek in your ear: scholarly battles are still raging, as they have since Shakespeare's time, over how to scan iambic pentameter in English —is it a matter of "longs" and "shorts," as in Greek, or is it all word stress?)

There are two major schools of thought on how Saturnian verse works. The first says that a standard line is a sequence of six "feet" with a break (or *caesura*) between the third and fourth. Each "foot" has two parts, the stressed (generally *first*) part, called a *thesis*; and the unstressed (generally *second*) part, called an *arsis*. The *thesis* is supposed to be either a single long-vowel syllable, or two shorts; the *arsis* is supposed to be either a long-vowel syllable, or two shorts, except sometimes it's just a single short. The other theory says that word stress is the thing and that longs and shorts don't really have anything to do with it except insofar as longs and shorts happen to be important factors in the determination of word stress in general. Again, two syllables can stand for one if they're unstressed.

The following is a couplet only in that the second line was the response to the first, but both are generally agreed to be in the same meter, namely, Saturnian. The author of the first line was one Naevius, who lived in the last quarter of the third century B.C. during the political ascendancy of some people of the *gēns Metellus*, whom Naevius would have us think *Matellae* instead of *Metellī*. (His fairly tame remark quoted here and others apparently less so about the *Metellī* landed him in jail eventually, but, then, one of the laws of the Twelve Tables says that you can be clubbed to death for singing scurrilous songs about people, so perhaps imprisonment was justly considered to be fairly mild punishment for such an offense.) The second line of the sample is the response of one *Metellus*:

Fātō Metellī Rōmae fīunt cōnsulēs.
Dabunt malum Metellī Naeviō Poetae.

It's only by blind luck that the Metelli ever got to be consuls of Rome. / The Metelli are going to give the poet Naevius a hard time (a bad thing).

Even allowing for the fact that a vowel plus two or more consonants counted as long, as did a diphthong, and you could fiddle with the number of syllables in a line by calling words like *Naeviō*, in which you have two unstressed vowels next to each other, trisyllabic (*Nae-vi-ō*) or disyllabic (*Nae-viō*) according to what you needed, neither of the general theories of what made the Saturnian meter tick is totally adequate. But since there are only a handful of lines of Saturnian that have come down to us, we will probably never know the full story.

Nor did any linguist or literary critic during the days when people still regularly wrote in Latin think to explain the Saturnian system for later generations. The reason for this oversight was undoubtedly in large measure that Greek meters had very early taken over as the ones to write in and anyone writing in the apparently native Latin Saturnian was considered an oaf, unworthy of attention.

Classical Greek meters, which generally work just fine if you look at them as different kinds of long-vowel, short-vowel sequences, were easily taken over into Latin. A favorite proved to be dactylic (heroic) hexameters, of which an example is given here from Ovid's *Metamorphoses* (completed in A.D. 8, shortly before its author was sent into exile for some grave offense, the precise nature of which remains unclear).

A standard line of dactylic hexameter is a sequence of six feet, with a *caesura* in the middle of the third foot. Each foot is supposed to be a sequence of a long plus two shorts or a long plus a long. The final vowel in a line is considered long or short as desired. The overall effect has been described variously as "like a waltz" or "like running with a basketball firmly attached to the sole of one of your feet." Judge for yourself:

Īnstruit et nātum, "Mediō" que "ut līmite currās,
Īcare," ait; "Moneō nē, sī dēmissior ībis,
Unda gravet pennās, sī celsior, ignis adūrat."

And he outfits his son. "You'd better stick to the middle path, / Icarus; I'm warning you, if you go too low, / The water (a wave) might weigh your feathers down, if too high, the sun (fire) might burn them." Icarus and his father, Daedalus, are at this point in the story about to escape from Crete with the help of some home-made wings.

Here, too, it helps to remember that diphthongs and vowels occurring before two or more consonants count as long. Actually, a consonant plus "r" can count as a single consonant, as is demonstrated in the second line of the following, the upshot of the Daedalus-Icarus story. Notice, in the next-to-last line, the elision of the two contiguous vowels, which is a common though by no means obligatory convention in Latin versification.

Cūm pŭĕr | āudā\cĭ cŏĕ\pĭt gaū\dērĕ vŏ\lātū
Dēsĕrŭ\ĭtquĕ dŭ\cēm, cāe\lĭquĕ cŭ\pĭdĭnĕ | trāctūs,
Āltĭŭs | ēgĭt ĭ\tēr. Răpĭ\dĭ vĭ\cīnĭă | sōlĭs
Mōllĭt ŏ\dōrā\tās pēn\nārūm | vīncŭlă | cērās.
Tābŭĕ\rānt cē\rāe. Nū\dōs quătĭt | īllĕ lă\cērtōs;
Rēmĭgĭ\ōquĕ că\rēns, nōn | ūllās | pērcĭpĭt | aūrās;
Ōrăquĕ | cāerŭlĕ\ā pătrĭ\ŭm clā\māntĭă | nōmēn
Ēxcĭpĭ\ūntŭr ă\quā, quāe | nōmēn | trāxĭt ăb | īllō.
Āt pătĕr | īnfē\līx, nĕc | iām pătĕr | "Īcărĕ" | dīxĭt,
"Īcărĕ," | dīxĭt, "Ū\bĭēs? Quā | tē rĕgĭ\ōnĕ rĕ\quīrām?"
"Īcărĕ" | dīcē\bāt, pēn\nās ā\spēxĭt ĭn | ūndĭs. . . .

When the boy began to rejoice in bold flight / He deserted the leader and, drawn by desire for the sky, / Made his way higher. Proximity to the fierce sun / Softened the fragrant wax, the binding of the feathers. / The wax had melted. He shook his bare arms / And, lacking an oarage, he caught no breezes; / And his lips, crying the name of his forefathers / Are snatched by the sky-blue water which took its name from him. / And the unhappy father, not now a father, said "Icarus. / "Icarus," he said, "where are you? In what region might I seek you?" / "Icarus," he was saying, (when) he saw the feathers on the waves.

Greek meters ultimately lost their utility, basically because Latin quit distinguishing between long and short, trading in its old vocalic system for a newer model that only made timbre distinctions. Soon people began to forget what used to be long and short, which made writing in the classical meters rather hard without a dictionary. The result in late Latin is verse that is based on different patterns of word stress and throws in rhyme to boot. An example of late Latin verse is given at the end of this chapter.

Vocabulary

imprimō, imprimere, impressī, impressum to press upon, imprint

fīdō, fīdere, fīsus sum to trust

fātum, fātī (n.) fate, calamity

fīō, fierī, factus sum to be made, be done, to become. *Fīō* is irregular in its conjugation: present indicative: *fīō, fīs, fit, fīmus, fītis, fiunt*; imperfect indicative: *fīēbam, fīēbās*, etc.; future: *fīam, fīēs*, etc.; the perfect, pluperfect, and future perfect are made with the past participle, *factus (-a, -um)*, and the appropriate form of *esse: factus (-a, -um) sum*, etc.; *factus (-a, -um) eram*, etc.; *factus (-a, -um) erō*, etc.; present subjunctive: *fīam, fīās*, etc.; imperfect subjunctive: *fierem, fierēs*,

etc.; the perfect and pluperfect subjunctive are again made with *factus (-a, -um)* plus the appropriate forms of *esse: factus (-a, -um) sim*, etc.; and *factus (-a, -um) essem*, etc.

cōnsul, cōnsulis (m.) consul

poēta, poētae (m.) poet

īnstruō, īnstruere, īnstrūxī, īnstrūctum outfit, equip, instruct

līmes, līmitis (m.) path, course

āiō, ais, ait, āiunt . . . to affirm, say. Like *inquam, āiō* is defective.

moneō, monēre, monuī, monitum to warn, admonish

dēmissus, dēmissa, dēmissum low

gravō, gravāre, gravāvī, gravātum to weigh down

penna, pennae (f.) feather

127

celsus, celsa, celsum high, elevated

puer, pueri (m.) boy

audāx (gen. *audācis*) bold

coepere, coepi, coeptum to begin (another defective verb)

gaudeō, gaudēre, gāvisus sum to rejoice, be happy

volō, volāre, volāvi, volātūrus to fly; *volatus, volatūs* (m.) flight

dēserō, dēserere, dēserui, dēsertum to desert, leave

dux, ducis (m.) leader; cf. *dūcō, dūcere* to lead

caelum, caeli (n.) sky, heaven

cupīdō, cupīdinis (f.) desire, greed

trahō, trahere, trāxi, tractum to draw, drag, haul

altus, alta, altum high, lofty

agō, agere, ēgi, āctum to move, lead, act; *iter agere* to make one's way

rapidus, rapida, rapidum fierce, impetuous, swift

vicīnia, vicīniae (f.) vicinity, neighborhood

sōl, sōlis (m.) sun

molliō, mollīre, mollīvi, mollītum to soften

odōrātus, odōrāta, odōrātum fragrant

vinculum, vinculi (n.) binding, fetter

tābeō, tābēre, ——, —— to melt away, waste away

lacertus, lacerti (m.) arm

rēmigium, rēmigii (n.) oarage, rowing apparatus

careō, carēre, carui, caritūrus to lack; the thing lacked appears in the ablative

percipiō, percipere, percēpi, perceptum to catch, collect

aura, aurae (f.) air, breeze

ōs, ōris (n.) mouth, face; (pl.) lips

caeruleus, caerulea, caeruleum sky-blue

excipiō, excipere, excēpi, exceptum to take up, catch

aqua, aquae (f.) water

iam now; cf. *heri* yesterday and *crās* tomorrow

regiō, regiōnis (f.) region, direction

requirō, requirere, requisivi, requisitum to search for

doceō, docēre, docui, doctum to teach, instruct; *Docti*, having been taught, are sages.

convocō, convocāre, convocāvi, convocātum to call together

Germānus, Germāna, Germānum German, the Germans being but one of the many Germanic tribes with whom the later Romans were acquainted if not very friendly.

adsum, adesse, adfuī, adfutūrus
to be present
sapiēns, sapientis knowing,
knowledgeable (from *sapiō,*
sapere, sapīvī, —— to taste,
know)
sermō, sermōnis (m.) speech,
discourse
Visigothus, Visigotha, Visi-
gothum Visigoth, another
of the Germanic tribes
quīdam, quaedam, quoddam
(like *quī, quae, quod*, only
with *-dam* stuck onto the
end) a certain
inveniō, invenīre, invēnī, inven-
tum to come upon, come
up with, invent

vir, virī (m.) man
per through, by (with the
accusative)
sīdus, sīderis (n.) constellation;
pl. stars, heavens
mittō, mittere, mīsī, mīssum
to send
Hispānus, Hispāna, Hispānum
Spanish
sēdēs, sēdis (f.) seat, chair
exsiliō, exsilīre, exsiluī, ——to
spring forth, leap up
subitō suddenly
tūtus, tūta, tūtum safe
carpō, carpere, carpsī, carptum
to pick, snatch; navigate
along

Fābula

Sunt in universitate
Docti Galli et Britanni
Convocati et Germani;
Adfuerunt sapientes
    Mundi Totius,

Ad sermonem auditum
Visigothi cuiusdam
Narraturus qui erat
    Mirabilia.

"Modum invenimus
Virum per caeruleum
Iactandi ad sidera;
primum mittemus hunc
    Ad solem ipsum."

Doctus autem Hispanus
Ridens sede exsiluit
Subito, "Quomodo (inquit)
    Solis ignibus

Tutam carpat astronauta
Viam? Num de Daedalo (ait)
Visigothi audiverunt
    Antiquam fabulam?"

Visigothus doctus ait,
"Hominem facillime
Sic in caelum mittere:
    Nocte media!"

The Trots

Chapter II.

I. a. A war in France is bad, but a war in a chamber pot is horrible.
   b. The children of Bacchus are adulterers.
   c. The world is a suitable place for islands.
   d. The sailor gives the farmer a crab; the farmer (gives) the sailor an apple.
   e. The farmer's daughter gives good things of the fields to (her) father-in-law.
   f. The sailor's son is on the island; the island (is) under the chamber pot.
   g. The world of the adulterer is three-cornered.
   h. Britain is not a suitable place for a war.

II. a. *Īnsula locus nōn idōnea adulterō.*
    b. *Agrī sub agricolīs et mundus sub agrīs.*
    c. *Socer bona nōn dat adulterō.*
    d. *Librī bonī, sed līberī taetrī.*
    e. *In Britanniā, adulter puellīs bonōs librōs dat; sed in Galliā, cancrōs.*
    f. *O fīliī et fīliae Galliae, māla Britanniae taetra.*
    g. *Fīlius nautae in locō idōneō fīliīs nautārum.*
    h. *Gallia nōn īnsula triquetra.*

Chapter III.

I. a. The sailor sits to the right of the farmers.
   b. Apple trees don't have pears, but apples.
   c. You do not thank Rome for their abominable war, O farmers of Gaul.
   d. I am making the field three-cornered because of a pair of pear trees and an apple tree.

132

e. We are coming to Gaul but we aren't running.
f. You have a right; you have a left; you have a third that is neither: therefore you are three-cornered.

II. a. *Nautae glōriōsī semper in īnsulās current.*
b. *Pōmārium vidēre nōn potes (potestis) propter pōmōs.*
c. *Adulter bonus ambōbus grātiās agit: puellae et socerō.*
d. *Matella locus nōn idōneus pirō.*
e. *Taetrī estis, O fīliī et fīliae Britanniae, nōn idōneī matellae.*
f. *Bina māla ā mālō capiō.*

III. Fruit trees are not good.
An apple tree is a fruit tree.
An apple tree is therefore not good.

Chapter IV.

I. a. I hear either the rain on the walls or the feet of soldiers in the street.
b. Both chickens and pigs run into the streets of the foul city.
c. The names of the brothers are not famous; nor is the name of one more famous than the name of the other.
d. The nature of neither the world by itself nor of the universe as a whole is three-cornered.
e. I say "Hi" to the soldiers on the bridge and "Bye" to the farmers in the field.

II. a. *Vel in nocte vel in imbrī aut in turrim aut in pōmārium currere potes (potestis).*
b. *Agricola in agrō et nauta in marī nōn parēs.*
c. *Īnsulam tōtam ā turrī vidēre possum et tōta taetra est.*
d. *Trium animālium nōmina sunt: cancer, gallusque homō.*
e. *Ūnus bonus, alter malus, sed neuter triquetrus.*

III. Two men of a famous university in Gaul seek the nature of man. One says to the other, "Man alone is a featherless biped." The other doesn't answer then, but leaves the university. In the night, he comes back to the university and throws a plucked chicken over the wall.

Chapter V.

I. a. The universe isn't three-cornered, is it? *Minimē.*
   b. How can you be in two places at once when you're not anywhere at all? *Bīnī sum.*
   c. Why did the chicken cross the road? *Gallus trāns viam iit quia cerevisiam dēsīderābat.*
   d. Does he sit on the right or on the left of the father? *Vel ad dexteram, vel ad sinistram patris sedet.*
   e. Where's a good place for beer? *Locus idōneus cerevisiae est in cūpā.*

II. a. *Cerevisiam imperābam quandō ursus in tabernam introiit.*
   b. *Utrum "Māla dēsīderō" dīxit an "Mala dēsīderō"?*
   c. *Nōnne pira pōma (sunt)?*
   d. *Ubi erant nautae nisi in cūpīs?*
   e. *Unde vēnimus atque quō īmus?*

III. A bear went into a bar and ordered a beer. The bartender ran from the bar to his employer, saying, "Boss! Boss! There's a bear in the bar and he wants a beer!" The owner answered the bartender, "Dummy, do we sell beer or do we sell apples in the bar? You can sell the bear a beer and, because bears are stupid animals, you can then tell him 'The price is a *sestertium.*'"

The bartender went back in the bar and gave the bear a

beer, saying, "That'll be a *sestertium.*" The bear didn't answer but took the beer. The bartender said, speaking in the way bartenders do, "You don't see too many bears in a bar, do you?" "That's right," answered the bear. "You don't, un-doubtedly because of the outrageous price of the beer."

Chapter VI.

I. "Concerning the Two Water Clocks of Morbonia"
A friend was saying good-bye to a merchant. "I was in Sicily last year, in Morbonia, the city of my clan; since you're going to Sicily, go to the city of my clan. It's really pretty and in the square, there's a gorgeous old water clock."

The merchant went to Sicily in a ship and said to the helms-man, "I want to get off in my friend's city because there's a pretty old water clock in the square, or so he told me."

Thus he arrived at the square of the city of Morbonia: marvelous to tell, there was not only one water clock, but two! One said VII o'clock and other VI o'clock. The merchant went into a bar and asked the bartender, "Why are there two water clocks in the square? Why don't both of them either say VII o'clock or else VI o'clock?" The bartender answered the mer-chant, "It is precisely because they don't tell the same time that we need two water clocks."

II. a. Is $\overline{A}$ *fricānus* your nickname or your family name?
   b. In our city there's a water clock, but it's neither beautiful nor pretty.
   c. O fool! You arrived at the city of our clan without your shoes!
   d. Behold thou art fair, my beloved! Behold thou art fair!
   e. Since you have done good things for me, I'm giving you our water clock.

III.a. *Antiquae clepsydrae meae valedīxī in Morbōniā priōre annō.*
 b. *Opus est vōbīs gubernātōre, amīcī meī.*
 c. *Quārē mihi dedit calceōs tuōs piscātor?*
 d. *Tū sōlus amīcus es meus, o tabernārius.*
 e. *Opus est ambōbus cīvitātibus clepsydrā, amīca mea.*

Chapter VII.

I. a. *O sī matellam habuissent!*
 b. *Homō sit aut nōn sit, ut tabernā meā exeat.*
 c. *Sī in ōre tuō crescat mālus, ōs diūtius nōn habeās, sed pōmārium.*
 d. *Sī barbam haberet avia, avus esset.*
 e. *Sī cerevisiam nōn dēsīderāvisset ursus, in tabernam nōn ierit.*

II. The animals of the forest had been waiting for a long time in a cave because of the cold and excessive snow. A month went by and the animals began to get hungry. "I'm starving," said the bear. "Me too," said the ox. The wolf said, "Somebody should go out and bring us back some food." "Right on," said the snake. "Maybe you'd like to go out and bring us back some food." "No!" answered the other. "Let's cast lots," said the deer, "so that we might choose a delegate." Thus by lot they elected the turtle.

The turtle said good-bye to the animals and disappeared into the shadows of the cave. Several hours went by and the bear asked, "Where's the turtle? I'm starving!" "Me too," said the ox. "The turtle's been gone an awfully long time. If only we'd sent somebody faster," said the wolf and the snake as one. Then from the shadows near the door of the cave, they heard the voice of the turtle: "O friends, if you should thus speak ill of me, I should remain here in the cave."

Chapter VIII.

I. a. I am about to go to Morbonia by boat, as the trip is to be made. The trip is to be made this way because Morbonia is on an island.

 b. My hat, it has three corners,
 Three corners has my hat;
 If it didn't have three corners,
 It wouldn't be fit to eat.

 c. I shall go forth; you however will stay here to await my return.

 d. We shall be able to eat our shoes in winter, your shoes having been eaten in summer.

 e. If they arrive at night (if they shall have arrived at night), they'll have come by the Via Appia; if the next day, by the road from Morbonia.

II. a. *Sī petasus meus triquetrus nōn esset, avus esset.*

 b. *Sī homō hominem rogābit "Utrum ursus es an homō?" alter rārō respondēbit "Ursus sum."*

 c. *Sī bōs super lūnam saltāre nōn potest, caniculus rīdēre nōn poterit bovem vidēns super lūnam saltantem.*

 d. *Sī mīlitēs Viā Appiā ventūrī sunt, ūna lūcerna pendenda est in turris fenestrā.*

 e. *Sed sī Viā Morboniā ventūrī sunt, gallus dēnūdātus plūmīs super mūrum ūniversitātis iactandus est.*

III. "Where Is Alba Longa?"
 A pilgrim was going from Rome to Alba Longa. He arrived at a crossroads where he saw two men sitting dressed in the manner of Etruscans. Both having been greeted, the pilgrim asked, "Does the road on the right lead to Alba Longa?" One said, *"Crapšti."*
 The other explained, laughing, "My friend said 'Yes,' but, like everybody in the Etruscan land, he's a liar."
 Is the truth to be known by the pilgrim or not?

Chapter IX.

I. a. Caesar ordered a beer in this bar; Pythagoras, in that one.

b. If only his legions had gone to hell!

c. The foolish foot soldier was in that catapult.

d. Several horsemen went into these Gallic fields; others however ran into the orchard.

e. With the turtle as *lēgātus,* the deer will be in charge of this *manipulus,* you, O wolf, (will be in charge of) that one.

II. a. *Hōc turture vīsō, omnibus turturibus vīsīs.*

b. *Ursus idem in fābulā nōn eādem.*

c. *Hī ursī nōn eīdem, sed vērō frātrēs sunt.*

d. *Ille ursus nōn frāter eōrum, sed māter.*

e. *Legiōnēs gallicae in fossā sunt; illae tuī (vestrī, vestrum) sunt in mālō.*

III. Two foot soldiers of Caesar's legion were digging a trench. One said to the other, "Do you see the centurion on the rampart of the camp? I was asking myself, 'Why is he up on the rampart while we're digging in the trench?'" The other answered him, "I don't know. You should ask him."

The foot soldier went to the centurion and asked him, "Why are you standing on the rampart while we're digging in that trench?" The centurion answered him, "This is quite easily demonstrated." The centurion made a fist in front of the stockade, saying to the foot soldier, "Hit my fist as hard as you can." The foot soldier was about to hit the centurion's fist when the latter very quickly moved his fist. The foot soldier thus hit the stockade as hard as he could. Pain! The centurion said, "Now do you know why I'm standing up on top of the rampart while you're digging in the trench? I'm smart and you're stupid." "Yes," replied the foot soldier, and went back into the trench.

His friend asked him, "Did the centurion tell you why he's

up there on the rampart while we're digging in the trench?" "Indeed," the other answered him. "It is very easily demonstrated." And making a fist in front of his face, he said to his friend, "Hit my fist as hard as you can."

Chapter X.

I. a. Ask not what your country can do for you but, rather, for whom the bell tolls.
   b. They said they were Etruscans, but they are undoubtedly liars.
   c. "I wrote what I wrote."
   d. If anybody asks, "Who is that?" answer "Nobody"; if (anybody asks) "What is he doing?" (answer) "Nothing."
   e. Oh I had a hat when I came in
      I hung it on a peg;
      And I'll have a hat when I go out
      Or I'll break somebody's leg.

II. a. *Dīxit culpam suam esse, sed nōn erat.*
    b. *Sī quis tē putet male mē dīxisse, Morbōniam adeat.*
    c. *Dīxērunt quod futūrum esse, futūrum esse; sed nōn erat.*
    d. *Hominī licet advocātum advocāre; lupō licet serpentem advocāre.*
    e. *In quā cūpā cerevisia mittenda est?*

III. The praetor said to three wrongdoers, "I will take you into a dark cave. In the cave (in which nothing can be seen because of the darkness), I will put hats on your heads. The hats which I shall put on your heads will be either black or white. Having put the hats on your heads, I'll go out. I will come back bearing a torch. If anyone sees a black hat, let him make a fist in front of his face. The first one to figure out what color his own hat

139

is will be allowed to leave: he will be a free man. Neither the second nor the third will be permitted to leave: they will remain in the cave forever."

So it happened. The torch having been brought, the three as one made fists in front of their faces. But nobody left, for nobody figured out the color of his own hat. Finally one of them ran for the door shouting "Hooray! Hooray!" What was the color of his hat?

Chapter XI.

I. a. If you were here, you'd be home.
   b. A bird in the hand and a beer in the hand are not the same.
   c. The hunter puts horns on the wall; adulterers, on the hunter's head.
   d. A foot soldier in the trench is better than two bears on the rampart.
   e. They came, it is easy to tell, for the purpose of greeting the bear, not for ordering a beer.

II. a. *Hī diēs bonī sunt, sed illī taetrī.*
    b. *Nōs mūtāvimus in cornibus.*
    c. *Cornua eius magna, sed ōs parvum.*
    d. *Bōzūs erāmus omnēs in hīs rēbus.*
    e. *Bōzo in īnsulā trēs imperātōrēs Rōmae sunt parēs.*

III. A man was walking with his large dog in the Via Appia. He saw another man who was approaching with a little ugly dog. The first man said to himself, "That guy with his little dog will step into the doorway of the shopkeeper so as to let me pass with my dog." But it was not thus. The men (with their dogs) came face to face. The little ugly dog bit the other's head off (ate the other's head). "?" cried the man. "A thing

140

easy to tell," said the man who had been walking with the little ugly dog. "My dog used to be a crocodile before I bobbed his tail and painted him (before the bobbing of his tail and the painting of him)."

Chapter XII.

I. a. "The bird, which is called 'bustard,' is good, but I don't think they have any here."
   b. It is a sweet and seemly thing to die for your country.
   c. It is a bitter and unseemly thing to be killed by Vesuvius.
   d. Those who do not shout are not heard; those who shout excessively however are not liked.
   e. Let him be seized who threw himself into the road.

II. a. *Illōs turturēs in illam tabernam sequāmur.*
    b. *Dūcantur in spēluncam.*
    c. *Nōn audiēbāris, o pedes, quia in fossā erās.*
    d. *Cerevisia imperātur in tabernā.*
    e. *Capientur ā nūllō.*

III. An evildoer dies and arrives in the underworld. Orcus says to the unhappy man, "There are three rivers in my kingdom. In one of them you will remain forever. You are however allowed to choose which one you will remain in. Come and see (that you might see) the rivers before choosing."

The dead man followed Orcus to the rivers. In the first, many were seen who cried out, shaking their bodies, "Don't come in this river! Don't come in here! The river's boiling wax!" In the second, many were seen who cried out and shook their bodies. "Don't come in this river! Don't come in here! The river's snow freezing with the cold!"

In the third, many were seen who murmured, not shaking

141

their bodies at all. "What's that?" the evildoer asked Orcus. "What are they saying?" "That's a river of dung," he answered. "They're saying, 'Don't make waves! Don't make waves!' "

Chapter XIII.

In the university
The learned Gauls and Britons
And the Germans were called together:
Sages were there
   Of the whole world,
To hear the discourse
Of a certain Visigoth
Who was about to tell of
   Wonders.
"We have discovered a way
"Of hurling a man through the blue
"To the stars;
"We shall send him first
   "To the sun itself."
But the Spanish sage
Laughing leapt from his seat
Suddenly, "How (he said)
   "From the fires of the sun
"Will your astronaut safely make
"His way? Of Daedalus (he said)
"Have the Visigoths not heard
   "The old tale?"
The learned Visigoth said,
"It is the simplest thing to send a man
"Into the heavens thus:
   "In the middle of the night!"

Ex Post Factō
or,
What to Do
Until Volume II
Arrives in the Mail

As we remarked in the preface (*Sicut erat in principiō*), there is always more. In the present case, of course, that includes again: if you liked this book, read it again. Further possibilities are as follows.

Acquire a good dictionary. An excellent investment is Lewis and Short's *A Latin Dictionary* (Oxford University Press, New York). The runner-up by at least a length is the slightly curtailed *A Latin Dictionary for Schools* by Lewis (same publisher and same Lewis). For English to Latin—and this is more useful than it might at first seem—we recommend *Cassell's New Latin Dictionary* (Funk and Wagnall, New York), and for postulating (and French-speaking) Indo-Europeanists, Ernout and Meillet's *Dictionnaire étymologique de la langue latine* (Librairie C. Klincksieck, Paris).

You may also wish to acquire a compendious reference grammar, such as Allen and Greenough's classic *New Latin Grammar for Colleges and Schools* (Ginn and Co., Boston). Such books are good to browse around in, and with a little patience and ingenuity, you can generally find an answer to even the obscurest of grammatical questions with illustrative examples from the classics for all occasions.

What then? Two tracks are worthy of mention. First, there is the traditional course of study: basic grammar, then Caesar's *Dē Bellō Gallicō*, then the *Aeneid* of Virgil, and possibly some Horace, Ovid, and Catullus, and perhaps a little prose. You have done the first and most difficult part (the grammar) if you have gotten anywhere near this far. All of these worthies and many others are available from the Oxford University Press (New York) and the Harvard University Press (in their Loeb Classical Library series, Cambridge), the latter with English trot (except where it's dirty, in which case, it's facing Latin and Latin, which at least tells you where the good parts are).

The traditional course has its reasons. Caesar's prose is sharp, clean, and not too hard, and has been greatly admired for centuries. There *is* an awful lot about the army in there, though perhaps no

more than you'd expect to find in a general's military memoirs. Virgil comes next because it's time for some poetry, if no less warring, and the *Aeneid* is all of that. Metrical verse tends to play hob with the syntax, which makes the *Aeneid* a little harder, though not much, especially if you've just warmed up on Caesar.

Much the same sort of thing may be said of Ovid and company, the Classical poets, and it is for this reason that they generally make their appearance only after most Latin students have given up and gone away, unalterably convinced that the true meaning of the dictum that you can't beat the classics is "Don't fool with them, they have you outnumbered."

There is an easier way: start with later Latin and work backward toward the authors of the Classical Age. If all roads eventually lead to Rome, why not, after all, take the route with the gentlest terrain—and much of the best scenery?

Easier than Caesar and infinitely more interesting is the *Biblia Sacra* (Desclée et cie., Paris). The translation of the Bible was undertaken in full appreciation of the fact that most of its readers would be at least a little shaky in their Latin and could use all the help they could get. As a result, the *Biblia Sacra* remains one of the most readily accessible Latin texts we have.

Also recommended is Harrington's superb collection, *Mediaeval Latin* (University Press of Chicago, Chicago), which has practically everything under the Medieval Latin sun in it in varying degrees of difficulty. From here, if you still want to read some Caesar or try your hand at something a little more ornate, you should encounter no great difficulty.

Or you could simply take the money and run.

Synopsis of the Grammar

NŌMINA

NOM	īnsula	mundus	bellum	ager	adulter
VOC	īnsula	munde	bellum	ager	adulter
GEN	īnsulae	mundī	bellī	agrī	adulterī
DAT	īnsulae	mundō	bellō	agrō	adulterō
ACC	īnsulam	mundum	bellum	agrum	adulterum
ABL	īnsulā	mundō	bellō	agrō	adulterō

PLURAL

NOM	īnsulae	mundī	bella	agrī	adulterī
VOC	īnsulae	mundī	bella	agrī	adulterī
GEN	īnsulārum	mundōrum	bellōrum	agrōrum	adulterōrum
DAT	īnsulīs	mundīs	bellīs	agrīs	adulterīs
ACC	īnsulās	mundōs	bella	agrōs	adulterōs
ABL	īnsulīs	mundīs	bellīs	agrīs	adulterīs

insula (f.) island; *mundus* (m.) world; *bellum* (n.) war; *ager* (m.) field; *adulter* (m.) adulterer.

SINGULAR

	MASC	FEM	NEUT	MASC	FEM	NEUT
NOM	bonus	bona	bonum	taeter	taetra	taetrum
VOC	bone	bona	bonum	taeter	taetra	taetrum
GEN	bonī	bonae	bonī	taetrī	taetrae	taetrī
DAT	bonō	bonae	bonō	taetrō	taetrae	taetrō
ACC	bonum	bonam	bonum	taetrum	taetram	taetrum
ABL	bonō	bonā	bonō	taetrō	taetrā	taetrō

PLURAL

	MASC	FEM	NEUT	MASC	FEM	NEUT
NOM	bonī	bonae	bona	taetrī	taetrae	taetra
VOC	bonī	bonae	bona	taetrī	taetrae	taetra
GEN	bonōrum	bonārum	bonōrum	taetrōrum	taetrārum	taetrōrum
DAT	bonīs	bonīs	bonīs	taetrīs	taetrīs	taetrīs
ACC	bonōs	bonās	bona	taetrōs	taetrās	taetra
ABL	bonīs	bonīs	bonīs	taetrīs	taetrīs	taetrīs

	SINGULAR			PLURAL		
NOM	līber	lībera	līberum	līberī	līberae	lībera
VOC	līber	lībera	līberum	līberī	līberae	lībera
GEN	līberī	līberae	līberī	līberōrum	līberārum	līberōrum
DAT	līberō	līberae	līberō	līberīs	līberīs	līberīs
ACC	līberum	līberam	līberum	līberōs	līberās	lībera
ABL	līberō	līberā	līberō	līberīs	līberīs	līberīs

bonus, bona, bonum good; *taeter, taetra, taetrum* foul; *līber, lībera, līberum* free.

SINGULAR

NOM	mīles	nōmen	turris	animal	mare	urbs
GEN	mīlitis	nōminis	turris	animālis	maris	urbis
DAT	mīlitī	nōminī	turrī	animālī	marī	urbī
ACC	mīlitem	nōmen	turrim	animal	mare	urbem
ABL	mīlite	nōmine	turrī	animālī	marī	urbe

PLURAL

NOM	mīlitēs	nōmina	turrēs	animālia	maria	urbēs
GEN	mīlitum	nōminum	turrium	animālium	marium	urbium
DAT	mīlitibus	nōminibus	turribus	animālibus	maribus	urbibus
ACC	mīlitēs	nōmina	turrīs	animālia	maria	urbēs
ABL	mīlitibus	nōminibus	turribus	animālibus	maribus	urbibus

mīles (m.) soldier; *nōmen* (n.) noun, name; *turris* (f.) tower; *animal* (n.) animal; *mare* (n.) sea; *urbs* (f.) city.

	SINGULAR			PLURAL		
	MASC	**FEM**	**NEUT**	**MASC**	**FEM**	**NEUT**
NOM	celeber	celebris	celebre	celebrēs	celebrēs	celebria
GEN	celebris	celebris	celebris	celebrium	celebrium	celebrium
DAT	celebrī	celebrī	celebrī	celebribus	celebribus	celebribus
ACC	celebrem	celebrem	celebre	celebrēs	celebrēs	celebria
ABL	celebrī	celebrī	celebrī	celebribus	celebribus	celebribus

	MASC-FEM	NEUT	MASC-FEM	NEUT
NOM	celebrior	celebrius	implūmis	implūme
GEN	celebriōris	celebriōris	implūmis	implūmis
DAT	celebriōrī	celebriōrī	implūmī	implūmī
ACC	celebriōrem	celebrius	implūmem	implūme
ABL	celebriōre	celebriōre	implūmī	implūmī

PLURAL

	MASC-FEM	NEUT	MASC-FEM	NEUT
NOM	celebriōrēs	celebriōra	implūmēs	implūmia
GEN	celebriōrum	celebriōrum	implūmium	implūmium
DAT	celebriōribus	celebriōribus	implūmibus	implūmibus
ACC	celebriōrēs	celebriōra	implūmēs	implūmia
ABL	celebriōribus	celebriōribus	implūmibus	implūmibus

	SINGULAR		PLURAL	
NOM	pār	pār	parēs	paria
GEN	paris	paris	parium	parium
DAT	parī	parī	paribus	paribus
ACC	parem	pār	parēs	paria
ABL	parī	parī	paribus	paribus

celeber, celebris, celebre famous; *celebrior, celebrius* more famous; *implūmis, implūme* featherless; *pār* equal, even.

	MASC	FEM	NEUT	MASC	FEM	NEUT
NOM	ūnus	ūna	ūnum	duo	duae	duo
GEN	ūnīus	ūnīus	ūnīus	duōrum	duārum	duōrum
DAT	ūnī	ūnī	ūnī	duōbus	duābus	duōbus
ACC	ūnum	ūnam	ūnum	duōs	duās	duo
ABL	ūnō	ūnā	ūnō	duōbus	duābus	duōbus

	MASC-FEM	NEUT
NOM	trēs	tria
GEN	trium	trium
DAT	tribus	tribus
ACC	trēs	tria
ABL	tribus	tribus

ūnus, ūna, ūnum one; *duo, duae, duo* two; *trēs, tria* three.

NOM	manus	cornū	diēs
GEN	manūs	cornūs	diēī (diē)
DAT	manuī (manū)	cornū	diēī (diē)
ACC	manum	cornū	diem
ABL	manū	cornū	diē

PLURAL

NOM	manūs	cornua	diēs
GEN	manuum	cornuum	diērum
DAT	manibus	cornibus	diēbus
ACC	manūs	cornua	diēs
ABL	manibus	cornibus	diēbus

manus (f.) hand; *cornū* (n.) horn; *diēs* (f.) day.

PRŌNŌMINA

	SINGULAR	PLURAL		SINGULAR	PLURAL
NOM	ego	tū		nōs	vōs
GEN	meī	tuī		nostrum	vestrum
				nostrī	vestrī
DAT	mihi	tibi		nōbis	vōbis
ACC	mē	tē		nōs	vōs
ABL	mē	tē		nōbis	vōbis

ego I, myself; *tū* you, yourself; *nōs* we, ourselves; *vōs* you, yourselves.

SINGULAR

	MASC	FEM	NEUT	MASC-FEM	NEUT
NOM	quī	quae	quod	quis	quid
GEN	cuius	cuius	cuius	cuius	cuius
DAT	cui	cui	cui	cui	cui
ACC	quem	quam	quod	quem	quid
ABL	quō	quā	quō	quō	quō

150

PLURAL

NOM	quī	quae	quae	quī	quae	quae
GEN	quōrum	quārum	quōrum	quōrum	quārum	quōrum
DAT	quibus	quibus	quibus	quibus	quibus	quibus
ACC	quōs	quās	quōs	quōs	quās	quōs
ABL	quibus	quibus	quibus	quibus	quibus	quibus

quī, quae, quod who, which; *quis, quid* who?, which?

SINGULAR

	MASC	FEM	NEUT	MASC	FEM	NEUT
NOM	hic	haec	hoc	ille	illa	illud
GEN	huius	huius	huius	illīus	illīus	illīus
DAT	huic	huic	huic	illī	illī	illī
ACC	hunc	hanc	hoc	illum	illam	illud
ABL	hōc	hāc	hōc	illō	illā	illō

PLURAL

NOM	hī	hae	haec	illī	illae	illa
GEN	hōrum	hārum	hōrum	illōrum	illārum	illōrum
DAT	hīs	hīs	hīs	illīs	illīs	illīs
ACC	hōs	hās	haec	illōs	illās	illa
ABL	hīs	hīs	hīs	illīs	illīs	illīs

SINGULAR				PLURAL		
NOM	is	ea	id	eī	eae	ea
GEN	eius	eius	eius	eōrum	eārum	eōrum
DAT	eī	eī	eī	eīs	eīs	eīs
ACC	eum	eam	id	eōs	eās	ea
ABL	eō	eā	eō	eīs	eīs	eīs

hic, haec, hoc this, this one; *ille, illa, illud* that, that one; *is ea id* this, that, he, she, it.

151

VERBA

Infinitives

Note: Nobody is *really* sure which part of speech infinitives belong to even today. There has been general agreement that they are either nouns or verbs but probably not both, at least not simultaneously. The Latin infinitives seem to have started life as the locative case forms of nouns made from verbs. With the effective disappearance of the locative case in Latin, a new status was voted to the infinitive: it was considered to be a "mood" of the verb on a par with the indicative, the subjunctive, and the imperative. All that means, essentially, is that infinitives usually get listed with the verbs instead of with the nouns. We place them here, technically in the class *Verba*, but close enough to the egress for safety.

ACTIVE

PRESENT

rogāre	monēre	dīcere	facere	audīre

PERFECT

rogāvisse	monuisse	dīxisse	fēcisse	audīvisse

PASSIVE

PRESENT

rogārī	monērī	dicī	facī	audīrī

For the so-called perfect passive, future active, and future passive infinitives, which really aren't infinitives at all, but participles plus the infinitive of the verb "to be," see *Participia* below.

INDICATIVE ACTIVE

PRESENT

	1.	rogō	moneō	dīcō	faciō	audiō
SING	2.	rogās	monēs	dīcis	facis	audīs
	3.	rogat	monet	dīcit	facit	audit

152

		rogāmus	monēmus	dicimus	facimus	audīmus
PLUR	1.	rogāmus	monēmus	dicimus	facimus	audīmus
PLUR	2.	rogātis	monētis	dicitis	facitis	audītis
	3.	rogant	monent	dicunt	faciunt	audiunt

IMPERFECT

SING	1.	rogābam	monēbam	dicēbam	faciēbam	audiēbam
SING	2.	rogābās	monēbās	dicēbās	faciēbās	audiēbās
	3.	rogābat	monēbat	dicēbat	faciēbat	audiēbat
PLUR	1.	rogābāmus	monēbāmus	dicēbāmus	faciēbāmus	audiēbāmus
PLUR	2.	rogābātis	monēbātis	dicēbātis	faciēbātis	audiēbātis
	3.	rogābant	monēbant	dicēbant	faciēbant	audiēbant

PERFECT

		rogāvī	monuī	dīxī	fēcī	audīvī
SING	1.	rogāvī	monuī	dīxī	fēcī	audīvī
SING	2.	rogāvistī	monuistī	dīxistī	fēcistī	audīvistī
	3.	rogāvit	monuit	dīxit	fēcit	audīvit
PLUR	1.	rogāvimus	monuimus	dīximus	fēcimus	audīvimus
PLUR	2.	rogāvistis	monuistis	dīxistis	fēcistis	audīvistis
	3.	rogāvērunt	monuērunt	dīxērunt	fēcērunt	audīvērunt

PLUPERFECT

		rogāveram	monueram	dīxeram	fēceram	audīveram
SING	1.	rogāveram	monueram	dīxeram	fēceram	audīveram
SING	2.	rogāverās	monuerās	dīxerās	fēcerās	audīverās
	3.	rogāverat	monuerat	dīxerat	fēcerat	audīverat
PLUR	1.	rogāverāmus	monuerāmus	dīxerāmus	fēcerāmus	audīverāmus
PLUR	2.	rogāverātis	monuerātis	dīxerātis	fēcerātis	audīverātis
	3.	rogāverant	monuerant	dīxerant	fēcerant	audīverant

FUTURE

SING	1.	rogābō	monēbō	dīcam	faciam	audiam
SING	2.	rogābis	monēbis	dīcēs	faciēs	audiēs
	3.	rogābit	monēbit	dīcet	faciet	audiet
PLUR	1.	rogābimus	monēbimus	dīcēmus	faciēmus	audiēmus
PLUR	2.	rogābitis	monēbitis	dīcētis	faciētis	audiētis
	3.	rogābunt	monēbunt	dīcent	facient	audient

SING	1.	rogāverō	monuerō	dixerō	fēcerō	audīverō
	2.	rogāveris	monueris	dixeris	fēceris	audīveris
	3.	rogāverit	monuerit	dixerit	fēcerit	audīverit
PLUR	1.	rogāverimus	monuerimus	dixerimus	fēcerimus	audīverimus
	2.	rogāveritis	monueritis	dixeritis	fēceritis	audīveritis
	3.	rogāverint	monuerint	dixerint	fēcerint	audīverint

SUBJUNCTIVE ACTIVE

PRESENT

SING	1.	rogem	moneam	dīcam	faciam	audiam
	2.	rogēs	moneās	dīcās	faciās	audiās
	3.	roget	moneat	dīcat	faciat	audiat
PLUR	1.	rogēmus	moneāmus	dīcāmus	faciāmus	audiāmus
	2.	rogētis	moneātis	dīcātis	faciātis	audiātis
	3.	rogent	moneant	dīcant	faciant	audiant

IMPERFECT

SING	1.	rogārem	monērem	dicerem	facerem	audīrem
	2.	rogārēs	monērēs	dicerēs	facerēs	audīrēs
	3.	rogāret	monēret	diceret	faceret	audīret
PLUR	1.	rogārēmus	monērēmus	dicerēmus	facerēmus	audīrēmus
	2.	rogārētis	monērētis	dicerētis	facerētis	audīrētis
	3.	rogārent	monērent	dicerent	facerent	audīrent

PERFECT

SING	1.	rogāverim	monuerim	dīxerim	fēcerim	audīverim
	2.	rogāveris	monueris	dīxeris	fēceris	audīveris
	3.	rogāverit	monuerit	dīxerit	fēcerit	audīverit
PLUR	1.	rogāverimus	monuerimus	dīxerimus	fēcerimus	audīverimus
	2.	rogāveritis	monueritis	dīxeritis	fēceritis	audīveritis
	3.	rogāverint	monuerint	dīxerint	fēcerint	audīverint

PLUPERFECT

SING	1.	rogāvissem	monuissem	dīxissem	fēcissem	audīvissem
	2.	rogāvissēs	monuissēs	dīxissēs	fēcissēs	audīvissēs
	3.	rogāvisset	monuisset	dīxisset	fēcisset	audīvisset

PLUR	1.	rogāvissēmus	monuissēmus	dīxissēmus	fēcissēmus	audīvissēmus
	2.	rogāvissētis	monuissētis	dīxissētis	fēcissētis	audīvissētis
	3.	rogāvissent	monuissent	dīxissent	fēcissent	audīvissent

IMPERATIVE ACTIVE

PRESENT

SING	2.	rogā	monē	dīc	fac	audī
PLUR	2.	rogāte	monēte	dīcite	facite	audīte

FUTURE

SING	2.	rogātō	monētō	dīcitō	facitō	audītō
	3.	rogātō	monētō	dīcitō	facitō	audītō
PLUR	2.	rogātōte	monētōte	dīcitōte	facitōte	audītōte
	3.	rogantō	monentō	dīcuntō	faciuntō	audiuntō

INDICATIVE PASSIVE

PRESENT

SING	1.	rogor	moneor	dīcor	facior	audior
	2.	rogāris,	monēris,	dīceris,	faceris,	audīris,
		rogāre	monēre	dīcere	facere	audīre
	3.	rogātur	monētur	dīcitur	facitur	audītur
PLUR	1.	rogāmur	monēmur	dīcimur	facimur	audīmur
	2.	rogāminī	monēminī	dīciminī	faciminī	audīminī
	3.	rogantur	monentur	dīcuntur	faciuntur	audiuntur

IMPERFECT

SING	1.	rogābar	monēbar	dīcēbar	faciēbar	audiēbar
	2.	rogābāris,	monēbāris,	dīcēbāris,	faciēbāris,	audiēbāris,
		rogābāre	monēbāre	dīcēbāre	faciēbāre	audiēbāre
	3.	rogābātur	monēbātur	dīcēbātur	faciēbātur	audiēbātur
PLUR	1.	rogābāmur	monēbāmur	dīcēbāmur	faciēbāmur	audiēbāmur
	2.	rogābāminī	monēbāminī	dīcēbāminī	faciēbāminī	audiēbāminī
	3.	rogābantur	monēbantur	dīcēbantur	faciēbantur	audiēbantur

155

SING	1.	rogābor	monēbor	dīcar	faciar	audiar
	2.	rogāberis,	monēberis,	dīcēris,	faciēris,	audiēris,
		rogābere	monēbere	dīcēre	faciēre	audiēre
	3.	rogābitur	monēbitur	dīcētur	faciētur	audiētur
PLUR	1.	rogābimur	monēbimur	dīcēmur	faciēmur	audiēmur
	2.	rogābiminī	monēbiminī	dīcēminī	faciēminī	audiēminī
	3.	rogābuntur	monēbuntur	dīcentur	facientur	audientur

The Passive Periphrastic

Everybody who likes words should know about "periphrastic." Periphrasis, like its boon companion, the paraphrase, is simply another way of saying something when all you have at hand are spare parts. That, basically, is the idea behind the periphrastic tenses. In Latin, as in English (and certain other languages that prefer to remain anonymous), the periphrastic tenses are formed of a participle and an auxiliary ("helping") verb, usually the verb "to be," though "to have" and "to go" have been known to put in a full day too.

In Latin, the perfect, pluperfect, and future perfect of the passive are periphrastic tenses made with the verb "to be" (*esse*) plus the past participle. The past participle agrees in number and gender with the subject of the verb. Thus,

PERFECT

SING	1.	rogātus, -a, -um sum	monētus, -a, -um sum	
	2.	rogātus, -a, -um es	monētus, -a, -um es	
	3.	rogātus, -a, -um est	monētus, -a, -um est	
PLUR	1.	rogātī, -ae, -a sumus	monētī, -ae, -a sumus	
	2.	rogātī, -ae, -a estis	monētī, -ae, -a estis	
	3.	rogātī, -ae, -a sunt	monētī, -ae, -a sunt	
SING	1.	dictus, -a, -um sum	factus, -a, -um sum	audītus, -a, -um sum
	2.	dictus, -a, -um es	factus, -a, -um es	audītus, -a, -um es
	3.	dictus, -a, -um est	factus, -a, -um est	audītus, -a, -um est

156

PLUR	1.	dictī, -ae, -a sumus	factī, -ae, -a sumus	audītī, -ae, -a sumus
	2.	dictī, -ae, -a estis	factī, -ae, -a estis	audītī, -ae, -a estis
	3.	dictī, -ae, -a sunt	factī, -ae, -a sunt	audītī, -ae, -a sunt

PLUPERFECT

SING	1.	rogātus, -a, -um eram	monētus, -a, -um eram
	2.	rogātus, -a, -um erās	monētus, -a, -um erās
	3.	rogātus, -a, -um erat	monētus, -a, -um erat
PLUR	1.	rogātī, -ae, -a erāmus	monētī, -ae, -a erāmus
	2.	rogātī, -ae, -a erātis	monētī, -ae, -a erātis
	3.	rogātī, -ae, -a erant	monētī, -ae, -a erant

SING	1.	dictus, -a, -um eram	factus, -a, -um eram	audītus, -a, -um eram
	2.	dictus, -a, -um erās	factus, -a, -um erās	audītus, -a, -um erās
	3.	dictus, -a, -um erat	factus, -a, -um erat	auditus, -a, -um erat
PLUR	1.	dictī, -ae, -a erāmus	factī, -ae, -a erāmus	audītī, -ae, -a erāmus
	2.	dictī, -ae, -a erātis	factī, -ae, -a erātis	audītī, -ae, -a erātis
	3.	dictī, -ae, -a erant	factī, -ae, -a erant	audītī, -ae, -a erant

FUTURE PERFECT

SING	1.	rogātus, -a, -um erō	monētus, -a, -um erō
	2.	rogātus, -a, -um eris	monētus, -a, -um eris
	3.	rogātus, -a, -um erit	monētus, -a, -um erit
PLUR	1.	rogātī, -ae, -a erimus	monētī, -ae, -a erimus
	2.	rogātī, -ae, -a eritis	monētī, -ae, -a eritis
	3.	rogātī, -ae, -a erunt	monētī, -ae, -a erunt

SING	1.	dictus, -a, -um erō	factus, -a, -um erō	audītus, -a, -um erō
	2.	dictus, -a, -um eris	factus, -a, -um eris	audītus, -a, -um eris
	3.	dictus, -a, -um erit	factus, -a, -um erit	auditus, -a, -um erit
PLUR	1.	dictī, -ae, -a erimus	factī, -ae, -a erimus	audītī, -ae, -a erimus
	2.	dictī, -ae, -a eritis	factī, -ae, -a eritis	audītī, -ae, -a eritis
	3.	dictī, -ae, -a erunt	factī, -ae, -a erunt	audītī, -ae, -a erunt

SUBJUNCTIVE PASSIVE

PRESENT

SING	1.	roger	monear	dīcar	faciar	audiar
	2.	rogēris,	moneāris,	dīcāris,	faciāris,	audiāris,
		rogēre	moneāre	dicāre	faciāre	audiāre
	3.	rogētur	moneātur	dicatur	faciātur	audiātur

PLUR	1.	rogēmur	moneāmur	dīcāmur	faciāmur	audiāmur
	2.	rogēminī	moneāminī	dīcāminī	faciāminī	audiāminī
	3.	rogentur	moneantur	dīcantur	faciantur	audiantur

IMPERFECT

SING	1.	rogārer	monērer	dīcerer	facerer	audīrer
	2.	rogārēris,	monērēris,	dīcerēris,	facerēris,	audīrēris,
		rogārēre	monērēre	dīcerēre	facerēre	audīrēre
	3.	rogārētur	monērētur	dīcerētur	facerētur	audīrētur
PLUR	1.	rogārēmur	monērēmur	dīcerēmur	facerēmur	audīrēmur
	2.	rogārēminī	monērēminī	dīcerēminī	facerēminī	audīrēminī
	3.	rogārentur	monērentur	dīcerentur	facerentur	audīrentur

PERFECT

SING	1.	rogātus, -a, -um sim	monētus, -a, -um sim
	2.	rogātus, -a, -um sīs	monētus, -a, -um sīs
	3.	rogātus, -a, -um sit	monētus, -a, -um sit
PLUR	1.	rogātī, -ae, -a sīmus	monētī, -ae, -a sīmus
	2.	rogātī, -ae, -a sītis	monētī, -ae, -a sītis
	3.	rogātī, -ae, -a sint	monētī, -ae, -a sint

SING	1.	dictus, -a, -um sim	factus, -a, -um sim	audītus, -a, -um sim
	2.	dictus, -a, -um sīs	factus, -a, -um sīs	audītus, -a, -um sīs
	3.	dictus, -a, -um sit	factus, -a, -um sit	audītus, -a, -um sit
PLUR	1.	dictī, -ae, -a sīmus	factī, -ae, -a sīmus	audītī, -ae, -a sīmus
	2.	dictī, -ae, -a sītis	factī, -ae, -a sītis	audītī, -ae, -a sītis
	3.	dictī, -ae, -a sint	factī, -ae, -a sint	audītī, -ae, -a sint

PLUPERFECT

SING	1.	rogātus, -a, -um essem	monētus, -a, -um essem
	2.	rogātus, -a, -um essēs	monētus, -a, -um essēs
	3.	rogātus, -a, -um esset	monētus, -a, -um esset
PLUR	1.	rogātī, -ae, -a essēmus	monētī, -ae, -a essēmus
	2.	rogātī, -ae, -a essētis	monētī, -ae, -a essētis
	3.	rogātī, -ae, -a essent	monētī, -ae, -a essent

SING	1.	dictus, -a, -um essem	factus, -a, -um essem	audītus, -a, -um essem
	2.	dictus, -a, -um essēs	factus, -a, -um essēs	audītus, -a, -um essēs
	3.	dictus, -a, -um esset	factus, -a, -um esset	audītus, -a, -um esset
PLUR	1.	dictī, -ae, -a essēmus	factī, -ae, -a essēmus	audītī, -ae, -a essēmus
	2.	dictī, -ae, -a essētis	factī, -ae, -a essētis	audītī, -ae, -a essētis
	3.	dictī, -ae, -a essent	factī, -ae, -a essent	audītī, -ae, -a essent

IMPERATIVE PASSIVE

PRESENT

SING	2.	rogāre	monēre	dīcere	facere	audīre
PLUR	2.	rogāminī	monēminī	dīciminī	faciminī	audīminī

FUTURE

SING	2.	rogātor	monētor	dīcitor	facitor	audītor
	3.	rogātor	monētor	dīcitor	facitor	audītor
PLUR	2.	—	—	—	—	—
	3.	rogantor	monentor	dīcuntor	faciuntor	audiuntor

PARTICIPIA

PRESENT

NOM	rogāns	monēns	dīcēns	faciēns	audiēns
GEN	rogantis	monentis	dīcentis	facientis	audientis

PERFECT

rogātus, -a, -um   monitus, -a, -um   dictus, -a, -um   factus, -a, -um
audītus, -a, -um

FUTURE

rogātūrus, -a, -um   monitūrus, -a, -um   dictūrus, -a, -um   factūrus, -a, -um
audītūrus, -a, -um

159

GERUNDIVE

(a.k.a. FUTURE PASSIVE PARTICIPLE)

rogandus, -a, -um   monendus, -a, -um   dicendus, -a, -um   faciendus, -a, -um
audiendus, -a, -um

rogō, rogāre, rogāvī, rogātum to ask; *moneō, monēre, monuī, monitum* to warn; *dīcō, dīcere, dīxī, dictum* to say; *faciō, facere fēcī, factum* to do, make; *audiō, audīre, audīvī, audītum* to hear.

Alia

The other classical parts of speech—*Adverbia, Praepositiones, Conjunctiones,* and *Interjectiones* have very little to say for themselves, really, that hasn't already been said as plainly as the surviving grammarians could possibly have said it, or at least *have,* if it comes to that. Try the index.

Anomaliae

When grammarians say, as they have for at least two millennia, that language is "regular," that is, that you can make up a finite number of rules that will describe how it all works, they don't mean this to be taken absolutely literally. Or they shouldn't, anyway, because we all know better: some anomalies, some exceptions to the rules, are bound to come forward.

Latin, like all other languages in robust health, has its anomalies and irregularities. The most important inhabit the verb system. We will hit the high points here, namely, the verbs *esse* to be, *posse* to be able, *īre* to go, *velle* to want, and *nōlle* to *not* want. The other ringleaders (*ēsse* to eat, *ferre* to bear, and *fierī* to become, be made) are presented in sufficient numbers when they appear in the text to exempt them from repetition here.

Because *esse, posse, īre, velle,* and *nōlle* are in essence active—you can't, for example, be been able without severe strain—we will give only their active forms, those being all there are besides. (This rule too has a minor exception: there is a passive-looking infinitive *īrī* to the verb *eō, īre* to go, but let us leave sleeping dogs supine.) With no further ado:

160

INFINITIVES

PRESENT

| esse | posse | īre | velle | nōlle |

PERFECT

| fuisse | potuisse | īsse | voluisse | nōluisse |

INDICATIVE

PRESENT

SING	1.	sum	possum	eō	volō	nōlō
	2.	es	potes	īs	vīs	nōn vīs
	3.	est	potest	it	vult	nōn vult
PLUR	1.	sumus	possumus	īmus	volumus	nōlumus
	2.	estis	potestis	ītis	vultis	nōn vultis
	3.	sunt	possunt	eunt	volunt	nōlunt

IMPERFECT

SING	1.	eram	poteram	ībam	volēbam	nōlēbam
	2.	erās	poterās	ībās	volēbās	nōlēbās
	3.	erat	poterat	ībat	volēbat	nōlēbat
PLUR	1.	erāmus	poterāmus	ībāmus	volēbāmus	nōlēbāmus
	2.	erātis	poterātis	ībātis	volēbātis	nōlēbātis
	3.	erant	poterant	ībant	volēbant	nōlēbant

PERFECT

SING	1.	fuī	potuī	iī	voluī	nōluī
	2.	fuistī	potuistī	īstī	voluistī	nōluistī
	3.	fuit	potuit	iit	voluit	nōluit
PLUR	1.	fuimus	potuimus	iimus	voluimus	nōluimus
	2.	fuistis	potuistis	īstis	voluistis	nōluistis
	3.	fuērunt	potuērunt	iērunt	voluērunt	nōluērunt

PLUPERFECT

SING	1.	fueram	potueram	ieram	volueram	nōlueram
	2.	fuerās	potuerās	ierās	voluerās	nōluerās
	3.	fuerat	potuerat	ierat	voluerat	nōluerat

PLUR					
	1.	fuerāmus	potuerāmus	ierāmus	voluerāmus	nōluerāmus
	2.	fuerātis	potuerātis	ierātis	voluerātis	nōluerātis
	3.	fuerant	potuerant	ierant	voluerant	nōluerant

FUTURE

SING					
	1.	erō	poterō	ībō	volam	nōlam
	2.	eris	poteris	ībis	volēs	nōlēs
	3.	erit	poterit	ībit	volet	nōlet

PLUR					
	1.	erimus	poterimus	ībimus	volēmus	nōlēmus
	2.	eritis	poteritis	ībitis	volētis	nōlētis
	3.	erunt	poterunt	ībunt	volent	nōlent

FUTURE PERFECT

SING					
	1.	fuerō	potuerō	ierō	voluerō	nōluerō
	2.	fueris	potueris	ieris	volueris	nōlueris
	3.	fuerit	potuerit	ierit	voluerit	nōluerit

PLUR					
	1.	fuerimus	potuerimus	ierimus	voluerimus	nōluerimus
	2.	fueritis	potueritis	ieritis	volueritis	nōlueritis
	3.	fuerint	potuerint	ierint	voluerint	nōluerint

SUBJUNCTIVE

PRESENT

SING					
	1.	sim	possim	eam	velim	nōlim
	2.	sīs	possīs	eās	velis	nōlis
	3.	sit	possit	eat	velit	nōlit

PLUR					
	1.	sīmus	possīmus	eāmus	velimus	nōlimus
	2.	sītis	possītis	eātis	velītis	nōlitis
	3.	sint	possint	eant	velint	nōlint

IMPERFECT

SING					
	1.	essem	possem	īrem	vellem	nōllem
	2.	essēs	possēs	īrēs	vellēs	nōllēs
	3.	esset	posset	īret	vellet	nōllet

PLUR					
	1.	essēmus	possēmus	īrēmus	vellēmus	nōllēmus
	2.	essētis	possētis	īrētis	vellētis	nōllētis
	3.	essent	possent	īrent	vellent	nōllent

PERFECT

SING	1.	fuerim	potuerim	ierim	voluerim	nōluerim
	2.	fueris	potueris	ieris	volueris	nōlueris
	3.	fuerit	potuerit	ierit	voluerit	nōluerit
PLUR	1.	fuerimus	potuerimus	ierimus	voluerimus	nōluerimus
	2.	fueritis	potueuritis	ieritis	volueritis	nōlueritis
	3.	fuerint	potuerint	ierint	voluerint	nōluerint

PLUPERFECT

SING	1.	fuissem	potuissem	īssem	voluissem	nōluissem
	2.	fuissēs	potuissēs	īssēs	voluissēs	nōluissēs
	3.	fuisset	potuisset	īsset	voluisset	nōluisset
PLUR	1.	fuissēmus	potuissēmus	īssēmus	voluissēmus	nōluissēmus
	2.	fuissētis	potuissētis	īssētis	voluissētis	nōluissētis
	3.	fuissent	potuissent	īssent	voluissent	nōluissent

IMPERATIVE

PRESENT

SING	2.	es	—	i	—	nōli
PLUR	2.	este	—	ite	—	nōlite

FUTURE

SING	2.	estō	—	itō	—	nōlitō
	3.	estō	—	itō	—	nōlitō
PLUR	2.	estōte	—	itōte	—	nōlitōte
	3.	suntō	—	euntō	—	noluntō

PARTICIPIA

PRESENT

NOM	—	potēns	iēns	volēns	nōlēns
GEN	—	potentis	euntis	volentis	nōlentis

FUTURE

futūrus, -a, -um	—	itūrus, -a, -um	— —

sum, esse, fuī, futūrus to be; *possum, posse, potuī* to be able; *eō, īre, iī, itūrus* to go; *volō, velle, voluī* to want; *nōlō, nōlle, nōluī* to not

Glossary

ā, ab from (with the ablative), iii

ac and, iv

Acheron, -untis (m.) Acheron, a river in the underworld, xii

   ōrae Acheruntis regions of Acheron, i.e., the Underworld itself,
     xii

ad toward, to, at (with the accusative), iii

adferō, adferre, attulī, adlātum to bring (back), vii

adsum, adesse, adfuī, adfutūrus to be present, xiii

adulter, -erī (m.) adulterer, ii

adūrō, adūrāre, adūrāvī, adūrātum to burn, xii

adverbium, -ī (n.) adverb, i

advocātus, -ī (m.) lawyer, x

advocō, advocāre, advocāvī, advocātum to call, summon, x

aes, aeris (n.) bronze, copper, hence bell, cymbal, x

aestās, aestātis (f.) summer, viii

ager, agrī (m.) field, ii

agger, -eris (m.) rampart, ix

āgnōmen, -minis (n.) honorific surname, vi

agō, agere, ēgī, āctum to move, act, lead, iii, xiii

   iter agere to make one's way, xiii

    grātiās agere to give thanks, iii

agricola, -ae (m.) farmer, ii

āiō, etc. to say, affirm, xiii

Alba Longa, Albae Longae (f.) Alba Longa, city of Latium, viii

albus, -a, -um white, x

alius, alia, aliud other, ix

alter, altera, alterum the other, iv

altus, -a, -um high, lofty, deep, xiii

amārus, -a, -um bitter, xii

ambō, ambae, ambō both, iii

amīcus, -a friendly, hence as noun, friend, vi

amō, amāre, amāvī, amātum to love, vi

amor, amōris (m.) love, vi

animal, -ālis (n.) animal, iv

annus, -ī (m.) year, vi

ante before (with the accusative), xi

antīquus, -a, -um ancient, old, vi

appropinquō, appropinquāre, appropinquāvī, appropinquātum to draw near, xi

apud with, according to, at the house of (with the accusative), xi

aqua, -ae (f.) water, xiii

arō, arāre, arāvī, arātum to plough, iii

aspiciō, aspicere, aspēxī, aspectum to observe, behold, look at, xii

atque and, iv

atrōx (gen. *atrōcis*) atrocious, iv

audāx (gen. *audācis*) bold, xiii

audiō, audīre, audīvī, audītum to hear, iii

aura, -ae (f.) air, breeze, xiii

aut ... aut ... either ... or ... (exclusive), iv

autem on the other hand, however; moreover, viii

auxilium, -ī (n.) help; as plural, auxiliary troops, ix

avē! hail! hello!, iv

avetarda, -ae (f.) bustard (Gk. *Ōtis, Ōtidos*), xii

avia, -ae (f.) grandmother, vii

avis, avis (f.) bird, v

avus, -ī (m.) grandfather, vii

barba, -ae (f.) beard, vii

bellum, -ī (n.) war, ii

bīnī, bīnae, bīna two (of the same sort), a pair, iii

bipēs (gen. *bipedis*) two-footed, iv

bonus, -a, -um good, ii

bōs, bovis (m. or f.) ox, cow, vii

bōzō, bōzūs (m.) clown, xi

Britannia, -ae (f.) Britain, England, ii

caelum, -ī (n.) sky, heaven, xiii

caeruleus, -a, -um sky-blue, xiii

Caesar, -aris (m.) Caesar, ix

calceus, -ī (m.) shoe, vi

cancer, cancrī (m.) crab, ii

caniculus, -ī (m.) little dog, viii

canis, canis (m.) dog, v

capilla, -ae (f.) hair, v

capiō, capere, cēpī, captum to catch, seize, iii

caput, capitis (n.) head, x

careō, carēre, caruī, caritūrus to be lacking (the thing lacked is in the ablative), xiii

caritās, -tātis (f.) dearness, hence high price, v

carpō, carpere, carpsī, carptum to pick, snatch; to navigate along (a route), xiii

castra, -ōrum (n.) a camp (pl. *tantum*), ix

cāsus, cāsūs (m.) falling, hence case (gram.), ii, xii

    cāsus rēctus upright case, i.e., the nominative

    cāsūs obliquī oblique cases, i.e., all the others

    cāsus bellī occasion (for outbreak) of war

catapulta, -ae (f.) catapult, ix

cauda, -ae (f.) tail, xi

celeber, celebris, celebre (gen. *celebris*) famous, frequented, iv

    celebrior, -brius more famous; more frequented, iv

celerius more speedily, vii

celsus, -a, -um high, elevated, xiii

centuria, -ae (f.) company of 60 to 100 soldiers, ix

centuriō, -ōnis (m.) centurion (commander of a *centuria*), ix

cēra, -ae (f.) wax, xii

cerevisia, -ae (f.) beer, v

certē certainly; yes, v

cervus, -ī (m.) deer, stag, vii

cibus, -ī (m.) food, vii

cīvis, cīvis (m.) citizen, vi

cīvitās, -tātis (f.) community of citizens, body politic, hence city, vi

clāvus, -ī (m.) nail, peg, x

clepsydra, -ae (f.) water clock, vi
coepere, coepī, coeptum to begin, xiii
cōgnōmen, -minis (n.) last name, surname, vi
cohors, cohortis (f.) cohort (body of soldiers = 3 *manipulī* = 6
    centuriae = 360 to 600 men), ix
color, colōris (m.) color, x
cōmissimē most politely, v
condus, condūs (m.) storekeeper, xi
conglaciō, conglaciare, ——, —— to freeze, xii
coniunctiō, -ōnis (f.) conjunction, i, iv
cōnsul, cōnsulis (m.) consul, xiii
convocō, convocāre, convocāvī, convocātum to call together, xiii
coram facing, face to face with (with the ablative), xi
cornū, cornūs (n.) horn, xi
corpus, corporis (n.) body, xii
crapšti an Etruscan epithet, recorded but as yet untranslated, viii
crās tomorrow, xiii
crescō, crescere, crēvī to grow, increase, vii
crocodīlus, -ī (m.) crocodile, xi
crustulum, -ī (n.) cookie, little cake, xi
culpa, -ae (f.) fault, guilt, x
cum when, since (with the ablative), vi
cūpa, -ae (f.) cask, v
cupīdō, cupīdinis (f.) desire, greed, xiii
currō, currere, cucurrī, cursum to run, iii, v
custōdiō, custōdīre, custōdīvī, custōditum to guard, keep watch, x
custōs, custōdis (m. or f.) guard, keeper, x

dē from, about (concerning), v
decōrus, -a, -um fit, seemly, xii
dēmissus, -a, -um low, xiii
dēnique at last, x
dēnūdātus, -a, -um stripped, iv
dēscendō, dēscendere, dēscendī, dēscensum to get down, descend, vi
dēsiderō, dēsiderāre, dēsiderāvī, dēsiderātum to long for, wish, v

dēserō, dēserere, dēseruī, dēsertum to desert, leave, xiii

dēsignō, dēsignāre, dēsignāvī, dēsignātum to designate, name, xii

dexter, dextera, dexterum right, iii

dīcō, dīcere, dīxī, dictum to say, iv

diēs, diēī (m.) day, xi

diū for a long time, vii

   diūtius for a while longer

disco, discere, didicī to learn, figure out, x

dō, dare, dedī, datum to give, v

doceō, docēre, docuī, doctum to teach, instruct, xiii

   doctus, -a, -um sage

dolor, dolōris (m.) anguish, pain, ix

dominus, -ī (m.) master of the house, employer, v

domus, domūs (domī) (f.) house, xi

dūcō, dūcere, dūxī, dūctum to lead, viii

dulcis, dulce (gen. *dulcis*) sweet, pleasant, xii

dum while, ix

duo, duae, duo two, iii

dux, ducis (m.) leader, xiii

ecce! behold!, vi

edō, ēsse (edere), ēdī, ēssum (ēsum) to eat, viii

ego, meī I, vi

eō, īre, iī, (īvī), itūrus to go, vi

eques, equitis (m.) cavalryman; patrician with income of 5000+
   sestertiī/yr. and the right to wear a gold ring, ix

equus, -ī (m.) horse, ix

ergō therefore, consequently, iii

et and, ii

   et . . . et both . . . and, iv

etiam still; even; yet; also; indeed, iii

etrūscus, -a, -um Etruscan, viii

euge! great! far out! right on! horray! (etc.), vii

euhoe! hooray! (etc.), x

ēvānescō, ēvānescere, ēvānuī to vanish, viii

ex from, out from (with the ablative), v

exclāmō, exclāmāre, exclāmāvī, exclāmātum to cry out, exclaim, x

excipiō, excipere, excēpī, exceptum to take up, catch, xiii

exeō, exīre, exiī, exitum to leave, iv

explicō, explicāre, explicāvī, explicātum to unfold, explain, viii

exsiliō, exsilīre, exsiluī to spring forth, leap up, xiii

exspectō, exspectāre, exspectāvī, exspectātum to await, viii

fābula, -ae (f.) conversation, tale, story, v

    fābulāns (gen. *fābulantis*) talking, v

    fābulāre (late Latin) to talk, v

facilis, facile (gen. *facilis*) easy, ix

facillimē most easily, ix

faciō, facere, fēcī, factum to make, do, iii

famēlicus, -a, -um starving, vii

famēs, famis (f.) hunger, vii

famescō, famescere to become hungry, vii

famulus, -ī (m.) servant, vii

fatum, -ī (n.) fate, calamity, xiii

fax, facis (f.) torch, x

fenestra, -ae (f.) window, viii

feriō, ferīre, ——, —— to hit, smite, ix

ferō, ferre, tulī, lātum to bear, carry, vii

ferveō, fervēre, fervuī to boil, xii

fibra, -ae (f.) fiber, entrails, vii

fīdō, fīdere, fīsus sum to trust, xiii

fīlia, -ae (f.) daughter, ii

fīlius, -ī (m.) son, ii

fīō, fierī, factus sum to be made, done; to become, xiii

flūmen, -minis (n.) river, xii

fodiō, fodere, fōdī, fossum to dig, ix

    fossa, -ae (f.) trench, ditch, ix

foedus, -a, -um ugly, xi

fōrmōsus, -a, -um beautiful, vi

fōrmōsissimus, -a, -um most beautiful, vi

forsitan (*forsan*) perhaps, vii
fortis, forte (gen. *fortis*) strong, ix
   fortissimē most strongly, as hard as possible, ix
forum, -ī (n.) marketplace, public square, vi
frāter, frātris (m.) brother, iv
frīgus, frīgoris (n.) the cold, vii
friō, friāre, ——, —— to crumble, xi
funda, -ae (f.) sling, ix
fungus, -ī (m.) mushroom, viii

Gallia, -ae (f.) Gaul, France, ii
Gallicus, -a, -um Gallic, ix
gallus, -ī (m.) rooster, chicken, iv
gaudeō, gaudēre, gāvisus sum to be happy, rejoice, xiii
gēns, gentis (f.) clan, people, race, vi
genū, genūs (n.) knee, xi
genus, generis (n.) family, race, sort, i, iv
germānus, -a, -um German, xiii
gesta, gestōrum (n.) deeds, acts (*pl. tantum*), vii
gladius, -ī (m.) sword, ix
glōriōsus, -a, -um full of glory, hence braggart, iii
gravō, gravāre, gravāvī, gravātum to weigh down, xiii
gubernātor, -tōris (m.) helmsman, vi

habeō, habēre, habuī, habitum to have, iii
herī yesterday, xiii
hic, haec, hoc this, ix
hiems, hiemis (f.) winter, viii
Hispānus, -a, -um Spanish, xiii
homō, hominis (m.) man, iv
hōra, -ae (f.) hour, vi
hortor, hortārī, hortātus sum to urge, exhort, xii

iactō, iactāre, iactāvī, iactātum to throw, iv
iam now, xiii

171

īdem, eadem, idem same, ix
idōneus, -a, -um suitable, fit for (with the dative), ii
ille, illa, illud that (one), ix
imber, imbris (m.) rain, iv
immoderātus, -a, -um unrestrained, outrageous, v
impār (gen. *imparis*) unequal, odd, iii, iv
imperātor, -tōris (m.) general, commander (in chief), ix
imperō, imperāre, imperāvī, imperātum to order, v
implūmis, implūme (gen. *implūmis*) featherless, iv
imprimō, imprimere, impressī, impressum to imprint, press upon, xiii
in in, on (with the ablative); into, toward (with the accusative), ii
īnfēlīx (gen. *īnfēlīcis*) unhappy, xii
inquam, etc. to say, xii
īnstruō, īnstruere, īnstrūxī, īnstrūctum to outfit, equip; instruct, xiii
īnsula, -ae (f.) island, ii
interficiō, interficere, interfēcī, interfectum to kill, xii
interiectiō, -ōnis (f.) interjection, i, iv
introeō, introīre, introīvī, introitum to enter, go into, v.
inveniō, invenīre, invēnī, inventum to invent, to come upon or up
    with, xiii
ipse, ipsa, ipsum self(-same), that very (one), x
is, ea, id he/she/it, ix
iste, ista, istud that one by/near you; later, that (expletive deleted)
    one, ix
ita thus, yes, v
iter, itineris (n.) way, journey, march, iv
    iter facere/agere to journey, march

labia, -ōrum (n.) lips (*pl. tantum*), vii
lacertus, -ī (m.) arm, xiii
Latīnī, -ōrum (m.) the Latins, Latin-speakers, inhabitants of Latium, i, ii
Latīnus, -a, -um Latin, i, ii
Latium, -ī (n.) Latium, whence came the *Latīnī* (west-central on the
    Italian peninsula), i, ii
laxus, -a, -um relaxed, unrestrained, vii

172

legatus, -ī (m.) envoy, delegate, vii

legiō, -ōnis (f.) legion (=10 *cohortēs*, or 3,600 to 6,000 troops), ix

lēgō, lēgāre, lēgāvī, lēgātum to delegate, appoint, vii

lēx, lēgis (f.) law, x

līber, lībera, līberum free, ii

Līber, Līberī (m.) Bacchus, ii

līberī, -ōrum (m.) children, ii

licet, licēre, licuit it is permitted (+ dative of the person to whom
      the permission is granted), x

līmes, līmitis (m.) path, course, xiii

locus, -ī (m.) place, location, ii

lūcerna, -ae (f.) lamp, viii

lūcifer, lūcifera, lūciferum light-bearing, -bringing, viii

lūna, -ae (f.) moon, viii

lupus, -ī (m.) wolf, vii

    lupus in fābulā! Speak of the Devil!, vii

lūx, lūcis (f.) light, viii

magnus, -a, -um big, great, xi

malē badly, vii

malefactor, -tōris (m.) evildoer, x

mālum, -ī (n.) apple, ii

malus, -a, -um bad, ii

mālus, -ī (m.) apple tree, iii

maneō, manēre, mānsī to remain, v

manipulus, -ī (m.) company of men (=2 *centuriae*, 120 to 200), ix

manus, manūs (f.) hand, xi

mare, maris (n.) sea, iv

matella, -ae (f.) chamber pot, ii

māter, mātris (f.) mother, vi

medius, -a, -um middle, xi

    in mediās rēs into the fray, xi

mendāx, -ācis (m.) liar, viii

mensis, mensis (m.) month, vii

mercātor, -tōris (m.) merchant, vi

meus, -a, -um my, vi

mīles, mīlitis (m.) soldier, iv
  mīles glōriōsus braggart soldier, a stock character in Roman
    comedy, whence *Commedia dell'Arte*'s Il Capitano,
    Shakespeare's Sir Andrew Aguecheek, et al.

minimē not in the least; no, v

mīrābilis, mīrābile (gen. *mīrābilis*) marvelous, xi
  mīrābile dictū marvelous to say, vi
  mīrābile vīsū marvelous to see, vi

mīrus, -a, -um wonderful, amazing, vii

mittō, mittere, mīsī, missum to send, xiii

modus, -ī (m.) fashion, way, method, v

molliō, mollīre, mollīvī, mollītum to soften, xiii

moneō, monēre, monuī, monitum to warn, admonish, xiii

mōnstrō, mōnstrāre, mōnstrāvī, mōnstrātum to make plain, show, vi
  Hōram vii mōnstrat it says seven o'clock, vi

Morbōnia, -ae (f.) Plagueville, vi

morbus, -ī (m.) distemper, vi

morior, morī, mortuus sum to die, xii

multus, -a, -um many, xii

mundus, -ī (m.) world, ii

murmurō, murmurāre, murmurāvī to murmur, mutter, xii

mūrus, -ī (m.) wall, iv

mūtō, mūtāre, mūtāvī, mūtātum to change, xi
  mūtātis mūtandīs the things to be changed having been changed,
    xi

nārrō, nārrāre, nārrāvī, nārrātum to make known, narrate, vi
  ut mihi nārrāvit as he told me

nāscor, nāscī, nātus sum to be born, xii

nātūra, -ae (f.) nature, iv

nauta, -ae (m.) sailor, ii

nāvis, nāvis (f.) ship, vi

-ne? ? (noncommittal question-marker), v

nec . . . nec . . . neither . . . nor . . . , iv

174

necne . . . ? . . . or not?, v

nēmō , nūllīus, neminī, neminem, nūllō, -ā, -ō nobody, x

neuter, neutra, neutrum (gen. *neutrīus*) neither (of two), i, iii, iv

niger, nigra, nigrum black, x

nihil nothing, x

nimis very much, xii

    nimius very, *very* much, xii

nisi except, if not (with the accusative), v

nix, nivis (f.) snow, vii

nōlō, nōlle, nōluī to wish not, x

    nōlī/nōlīte don't!, x

nōmen, nōminis (n.) name (of the *gēns*), noun, i, ii, iii, iv, vi

    nōmen adiectīvum adjective, i

nōn not, ii

nōnne . . . ? . . . , isn't that so? (question-marker, expecting "yes"), v

nōnnūllus, -a, -um (gen. *nōnnūllīus*) some, several, vii

nōs, nostrum (*nostrī*) we, vi

noster, nostra, nostrum our, vi

nox, noctis (f.) night, iv

nūllus, -a, -um (gen. *nūllīus*) none, no . . . , iv

num I don't suppose that . . . ? (question-marker, expecting "no"), v

nunc now, ix

odōrātus, -a, -um fragrant, xiii

omnis, omne (gen. *omnis*) all, every, pl. everybody, viii

opus est to need, the needy in the dative case, the thing needed in
    the ablative; *opus est tibi cerevisiā* You need a beer, vi

ōra, -ae (f.) border, edge, region, xii

Orcus, -ī (m.) Orcus, a lord of the underworld; hence the underworld
    itself, xii

ōs, ōris (n.) mouth, face; pl. lips, vii, xiii

pār (gen. *paris*) equal, even, iii, iv

pars, partis (f.) part, portion, ix

participium, -ī (n.) participle, i, ii

partior, partīrī, partītus sum to share, xii

parvus, -a, -um small, xi

pater, patris (m.) father, v

patria, -ae (f.) fatherland, country, x

patricius, -ī (m.) patrician, nobleman, aristocrat, x

pedes, peditis (m.) foot soldier, infantryman, grunt, ix

pendō, pendere, pependī, pēnsum to (cause to) hang, viii

penna, -ae (f.) feather, xiii

per through, by (with the accusative), xiii

percipiō, percipere, percēpī, perceptum to catch, collect, xii

peregrīnus, -ī (m.) foreigner, pilgrim, viii

perficiō, perficere, perfēcī, perfectum to finish, accomplish, v

perpetuitās, -tātis (f.) perpetuity, x

perveniō, pervenīre, pervēnī to arrive; with *ad* plus accusative, to
    reach, vi

pēs, pedis (m.) foot, iv

petasus, -ī (m.) hat, viii

  petasātus, -a, -um wearing a hat, behatted, x

pīlum, -ī (n.) lance, javelin, ix

pingō, pingere, pinxī, pictum to paint, xi

pictus, -ī (m.) Pict, a Celtic people in Britain who went into battle
    with their bodies painted blue

pirum, -ī (n.) pear, iii

pirus, -ī (m.) pear tree, iii

piscātor, -tōris (m.) fisherman, vi

piscis, piscis (m.) fish, vi

plēbs, plēbis (f.) plebeian, commoner, x

plicō, plicāre, plicāvī, plicātum to fold, viii

plūma, -ae (f.) feather; pl. down, iv

poeta, -ae (m.) poet, xiii

pōmārium, -ī (n.) orchard, iii

pōmum, -ī (n.) fruit, iii

pōmus, -ī (m.) fruit tree, iii

pollūtus, -a, -um fouled, vii

pōnō, pōnere, posuī, positum to put, place, x

pōns, pōntis (m.) bridge, iv
porcus, -ī (m.) pig, swine, i, ii
porta, -ae (f.) door, gate, i, ii
possum, posse, potuī to be able, iii
praecīdō, praecīdere, praecīdī, praecīsum to cut off, xii
praenōmen, -minis (n.) first name, vi
praepositiō, -ōnis (f.) prefixing; preposition (cf. *pōnō*), i
praetor, -tōris (m.) praetor; magistrate, x
pretium, -ī (n.) price, v
prīmipīlus, -ī (m.) chief centurion, ix
prīmus, -a, -um first, x
prior, prius (gen. *priōris*) former, prior, vi
  priōre annō last year, vi
prō before, on behalf of, in front of (with the ablative), ix
prōmittō, prōmittere, prōmisī, prōmissum to send forth, v
  prōmissus, -a, -um let grow, long, v
prōnōmen, -minis (n.) pronoun, i, iv, vi
prope near (with the accusative) (cf. *appropinquō*), vii
propter for, because of (with the accusative), iii
proximō diē on the next day
puella, -ae (f.) girl, ii
puer, puerī (m.) boy, xiii
pugnus, -ī (m.) fist, ix. Whence are derived:
  pugna, -ae (f.) fight
  pugnāre to fight
  oppugnāre to (take by) storm
pulcher, pulchra, pulchrum pretty, vi
putō, putāre, putāvī, putātum to think, x

quadrivium, -ī (n.) four-way intersection, crossroads, i, ii
quaerō, quaerere, quaesī, quaesītum to seek, ask, iv
quaestor, -tōris (m.) quaestor, chief financial officer of legion, ix
quandō when, v
quārē why?, v
quatiō, quatere, quassī, quassum to shake, xii

queō, quīre, quiī to be able, vii
quī, quae, quod who, which; he-/she-/it- who, x
quia since, because, v
quīdam, quaedam, quoddam a certain, xiii
quis, quid who/what?; whoever/whatever; somebody, x
quō where to? whither, v
quōmodō how?, v
quoque too, also, vii

rapidus, -a, -um fierce, swift, impetuous, xiii
rārus, -a, -um scarce, rare, v
   rārō seldom, rarely, viii
reātus, reātūs (f.) sin, charge, vii
redeō, redīre, rediī, reditum to go back, v
   reditūrus, -a, -um about to return, viii
recipiō, recipere, recēpī, receptum to accept, receive, v
regiō, regiōnis (f.) direction, region, xiii
rēmigium, -ī (n.) oarage, rowing apparatus, xiii
removeō, removēre, remōvī, remōtum to remove, move back, withdraw, ix
requīrō, requīrere, requīsīvī, requīsītum to search for, xiii
rēs, reī (f.) thing, xi
resonō, resonāre, resonāvī, resonātum to resound, vii
respondeō, respondēre, respondī, responsum to answer, iv
rēx, rēgis (m.) king, xii
   rēgnum, -ī (n.) kingdom, realm, xii
rīdeō, rīdēre, rīsī, rīsum to laugh, viii
Rōma, -ae (f.) Rome, i, iii
rogō, rogāre, rogāvī, rogātum to ask, vi

sacer, sacra, sacrum sacred, profane
sagitta, -ae (f.) arrow, ix
saltō, saltāre, saltāvī, saltātum to jump, dance, viii
salūtō, salūtāre, salūtāvī to greet, v
sānctus, -a, -um sacred, vii

sapiō, sapere, sapīvī to taste; know, xiii

 sapiēns (gen. *sapientis*) knowing, knowledgeable, xiii

scrībō, scrībere, scrīpsī, scrīptum to write, x

secundus, -a, -um second (cf. *sequor*), x

sed but, ii

sedeō, sedēre, sēdī, sessum to sit, iii

 sēdēs, sēdis (f.) seat, chair, xiii

semper always, iii

sermō, -mōnis (m.) speech, discourse, xiii

sequor, sequī, secutus sum to follow, xii

serpō, serpere, serpsī to crawl, creep, vii

 serpēns (gen. *serpentis*) crawling, hence snake

sēstertium, -ī (n.) sestertium, the worth of 1½ copper *assēs*, v

sī if, vii

sīc thus, v

Sicilia, -ae (f.) Sicily, vi

 Siculī, -ōrum (m.) Sicilians, i

sīdus, sīderis (n.) constellation; pl. stars, heavens, xiii

silva, -ae (f.) forest, vii

 silvāticus, -a, -um forest-dwelling, wild, vii

sine without (with the ablative), vi

sinister, sinistra, sinistrum left, iii

socer, socerī (m.) father-in-law, ii

sōl, sōlis (m.) sun, xiii

solea, -ae (f.) sandal, vi

sōlus, -a, -um (gen. *sōlīus*) sole; alone, iv

solveō, solvēre, solvī, solūtum to free, loosen, dissolve, vii

sors, sortis (f.) lot, chance, vii

 sortēs dūcere to cast lots, vii

spēlunca, -ae (f.) cave, vii

stercus, -coris (n.) dung, excrement, xii

stō, stāre, stetī, stātum to stand, vi

 status quō ante bellum standing where it stood before the war, vi

stultus, -a, -um stupid, v

sub under (with the ablative), ii

subitō suddenly, xiii
suī him-/her-/itself, x
sum, esse, fuī, futūrus to be, iii
super above (with the accusative), ii
suus, -a, -um his/her/its own, x

tābeō, tābēre, ——, —— to melt/waste away, xiii
taberna, -ae (f.) inn, tavern, bar, v
    tabernārius, -ī (m.) proprietor of a tavern, inn, or bar, v
taeter, taetra, taetrum foul, abominable, noisome, ii
tempus, temporis (n.) time; tense, i, iv, v
tenebrae, -ārum (f.) shadows, darkness, vii
    tenebricōsus, -a, -um dark, x
terra, -ae (f.) earth, land, v
tertius, -a, -um third, iii
tōtus, -a, -um (gen. *tōtīus*) whole, all, iv
trahō, trahere, trāxī, tractum to draw, drag, haul, xiii
trāns across (with the accusative), v
trānscēdō, trānscēdere, trānscessī to go by, pass, vii
trēs, tria (gen. *trium*) three, iv
tribūnus, -ī (m.) tribune (elected plebeian official), ix
triquetrus, -a, -um three-cornered, ii
trivium, -ī (n.) three-way intersection, fork in the road, iv
tū, tuī you (sing.), vi
tunc then, at that time, iv
turris, turris (f.) tower, iv
turtur, turturis (m.) turtle (-dove), vii
tūtus, -a, -um safe, xiii
tuus, -a, -um your (sing.), vi

ubi? where?, v
ūllus, -a, -um (gen. *ūllīus*) any, iv
unda, -ae (f.) wave, xii
unde whence, where from, v
ūniversitās, -tātis (f.) universe, totality, university, iv

ūnus, -a, -um (gen. *ūnīus*) one, iv
  ūnā as one, vii
urbs, urbis (f.) walled town, city, iv
ursus, -ī (m.) bear, v
ut as; in order that; would that, vii
uter, utra, utrum which (of two), iv
utinam would that (past events), vii
utrum . . . an . . . ? . . . ? or . . . ? (which of two), v

valē! farewell! goodbye!, iv
valedīcō, valedīcere, valedīxī, valedictum to say farewell, vi
vallum, -ī (n.) stockade, ix
vallus, -ī (m.) pike, ix
vastō, vastāre, vastāvī, vastātum to (lay) waste (mil.), iii
vel . . . vel either . . . or (maybe both), iv
venātor, -tōris (m.) hunter, xi
vendō, vendere, vendidī to sell, v
veniō, venīre, vēnī, ventum to come, iii
verbum, -ī (n.) word, verb, i, ii
vereor, verērī, veritus, sum to fear, xii
vēritās, -tātis (f.) truth, viii
  vērō truly, v
vertō, vertere, vertī, versum to turn (around), viii
vester, vestra, vestrum your (pl.), vi
vestiō, vestīre, vestīvī, vestītum to dress, clothe, viii
Vesuvius, -ī (m.) Mount Vesuvius, whose eruption in A.D. 79 buried
    Pompeii and Herculaneum, xii
via, -ae (f.) way, road, viii
  Via Appia the Appian Way from Rome to Naples, viii
vicīnia, -ae (f.) neighborhood, vicinity, xiii
videō, vidēre, vīdī, vīsum to see, iii
vinculum, -ī (n.) fetter, binding, xiii
vir, virī (m.) man, xiii
Visigothus, -a, -um Visigoth, xiii
volō, velle, voluī to wish, want, x

volō, volāre, volāvī, volātūrus to fly, xiii
  volātus, volātūs (m.) flight, xiii
vōs, vestrum (vestrī) you (pl.), vi
vōx, vōcis (f.) voice, vii
vulgus, -ī (m.) the crowd, the people, the masses, i, ii

English–Latin

able *potēns* (gen. *potentis*)
to be able *queō, quīre, quiī; possum, posse, potuī*
abominable *taeter, taetra, taetrum*
about (concerning) *dē* (with the ablative)
about to return *reditūrus, -a, -um*
above *super* (with the accusative)
accept *recipiō, recipere, recēpī, receptum*
accomplish *perficiō, perficere, perfēcī, perfectum*
according to, *apud* (with the accusative)
Acheron *Acheron, Acheruntis* (m.)
across *trāns* (with the accusative)
to act *agō, agere, ēgī, āctum*
acts *gesta, -ōrum* (n.)
adjective *nōmen adiectīvum, nōminis adjectīvī* (n.)
admonish *moneō, monēre, monuī, monitum*
adulterer *adulter, adulterī* (m.)
adverb *adverbium, adverbiī* (n.)
affirm *āiō*, etc.
air *aura, -ae* (f.)
Alba Longa *Alba Longa, Albae Longae* (f.)
all *tōtus, -a, -um* (gen. *tōtīus*); *omnis, omne* (gen. *omnis*)
alone *sōlus, -a, -um* (gen. *sōlīus*)
also *etiam, quoque*
always *semper*

amazing *mīrus, -a, -um*
ancient *antīquus, -a, -um*
and *et; atque, ac*
anguish *dolor, dolōris* (m.)
animal *animal, animālis* (n.)
answer *respondeō, respondēre, respondī, respōnsum*
any *ūllus, -a, -um* (gen. *ūllīus*)
Appian Way *Via Appia, Viae Appiae* (f.)
apple *mālum, -ī* (n.)
apple tree *mālus, -ī* (m.)
appoint *lēgō, -āre, -āvī, -ātum*
approach *appropinquō, -āre, -āvī, -ātum*
aristocrat(ic) *patricius, -a, -um*
arm *lacertus, -ī* (m.)
arrive *perveniō, pervenīre, pervēnī*
arrow *sagitta, -ae* (f.)
as *ut, sīcut*
ask *rogō, -āre, -āvī, -ātum; quaerō, quaerere, quaesīvī, quaesītum*
as one *ūnā*
at *ad* (with the accusative); *apud* (with the accusative)
at last *dēnique*
atrocious *atrōx* (gen. *atrōcis*)
at that time *tunc*
at the same time *eōdem tempore*
auxiliary troops *auxilia, -ōrum* (n.)
await *exspectō, -āre, -āvī, -ātum*

Bacchus *Līber, Līberī* (m.)
bad *malus, -a, -um*
badly *malē*
bar *taberna, -ae* (f.)
barkeeper *tabernārius, -ī* (m.)
to be *sum, esse, fuī, futūrus*
bear *ursus, -ī* (m.)
to bear *ferō, ferre, tulī, lātum*

beard *barba, -ae* (f.)
beautiful *fōrmōsus, -a, -um*
because *quia*
because of *propter* (with the accusative)
become *fīō, fierī, factus sum*
become hungry *famescō, famescere,* ——
beer *cerevisia, -ae* (f.)
before *pro* (with the ablative); *ante* (with the accusative)
begin ——, *coepere, coepī, coeptum*
on behalf of *prō* (with the ablative)
behatted *petasātus, -a, -um*
behold! *ecce!*
to behold *aspiciō, aspicere, aspēxī, aspectum*
bell *aes, aeris* (n.)
big *magnus, -a, -um*
binding *vinculum, -ī* (n.)
bird *avis, avis* (f.)
bitter *amārus, -a, -um*
black *niger, nigra, nigrum*
body *corpus, corporis* (n.)
body politic *cīvitās, -tātis* (f.)
boil *ferveō, fervēre, fervuī*
bold *audāx* (gen. *audācis*)
border *ōra, -ae* (f.)
to be born *nāscor, nāscī, nātus sum*
both *ambō, ambae, ambō*
both . . . and . . . *et . . . et . . .*
boy *puer, puerī* (m.)
braggart *gloriōsus, -a, -um*
breeze *aura, -ae* (f.)
bridge *pōns, pōntis* (m.)
bring (back) *adferō, adferre, attulī, adlātum*
Britain *Britannia, -ae* (f.)
bronze *aes, aeris* (n.)
brother *frāter, frātris* (m.)

burn *adūrō, -āre, -āvī, -ātum*
bustard *avetarda, -ae* (f.)
but *sed*
by *per* (with the accusative)

Caesar *Caesar, -aris* (m.)
calamity *fātum, -ī* (n.)
call *advocō, -āre, -āvī, -ātum*
call together *convocō, -āre, -āvī, -ātum*
camp *castra, -ōrum* (n.)
carry *ferō, ferre, tulī, lātum*
case *cāsus, -ūs* (m.)
cask *cūpa, -ae* (f.)
cast lots *sortēs dūcere*
catapult *catapulta, -ae* (f.)
catch *capiō, capere, cēpī, captum; excipiō, excipere, excēpī,*
    exceptum; percipiō, percipere, percēpī, perceptum
cause to hang *pendō, pendere, pependī, pēnsum*
cavalryman *eques, equitis* (m.)
cave *spēlunca, -ae* (f.)
centurion *centuriō, -ōnis* (m.)
a certain *quīdam, quaedam, quoddam*
certainly *certē*
chair *sēdēs, sēdis* (f.)
chamber pot *matella, -ae* (f.)
chance *sors, sortis* (f.)
change *mūtō, -āre, -āvī, -ātum*
charge *reātus, -ūs* (f.)
chicken *gallus, -ī* (m.)
chief centurion *prīmipīlus, -ī* (m.)
children *līberī, līberōrum* (m.)
citizen *cīvis, cīvis* (m.)
city *cīvitās, -tātis* (f.); *urbs, urbis* (f.)
clan *gēns, gentis* (f.)
clothe *vestiō, vestīre, vestīvī, vestītum*

185

clown *bōzō, bōzūs* (m.)
cohort (of soldiers) *cohors, cohortis* (f.)
cold(ness) *frīgus, frīgoris* (n.)
collect *percipiō, percipere, percēpī, perceptum*
color *color, -ōris* (m.)
come *veniō, venīre, vēnī, ventum*
come upon *inveniō, invenīre, invēnī, inventum*
come up with *inveniō*, etc.
commander (in chief) *imperātor, -ōris* (m.)
commoner *plēbs, plēbis* (f.)
community of citizens *cīvitās, -tātis* (f.)
company of one hundred soldiers *centuria, -ae* (f.)
company of two *centuriae manipulus, -ī* (m.)
concerning *dē* (with the ablative)
conjunction *coniunctiō, -ōnis* (f.)
consequently *ergō*
constellation *sīdus, sīderis* (n.)
consul *consul, consulis* (m.)
conversation *fābula, -ae* (f.)
cookie *crustulum, -ī* (n.)
copper *aes, aeris* (n.)
country *patria, -ae* (f.)
course *līmes, līmitis* (m.)
cow *bōs, bovis* (f.)
crab *cancer, cancrī* (m.)
crawl, creep *serpō, serpere, serpsī,* ——
crocodile *crocodīlus, -ī* (m.)
crossroads *quadrivium, -ī* (n.)
crowd *vulgus, -ī* (m.)
crumble *friō, -āre,* ——, ——
cry out *exclāmō, -āre, -āvī, -ātum*
cut off *praecīdō, praecīdere, praecīdī, praecīsum*

dance *saltō, -āre, -āvī, -ātum*
dark *tenebricōsus, -a, -um*

186

darkness *tenebrae, -ārum* (f.)
daughter *fīlia, -ae* (f.)
day *diēs, diēī* (f.)
dearness *cāritās, -tātis* (f.)
deeds *gesta, -ōrum* (n.)
deep *altus, -a, -um*
deer *cervus, -ī* (m.)
delegate *lēgātus, -ī* (m.)
to delegate *lēgō, -āre, -āvī, -ātum*
descend *dēscendō, dēscendere, dēscendī, dēscensum*
desert *dēserō, dēserere, dēseruī, dēsertum*
designate *dēsignō, -āre, -āvī, -ātum*
desire *cupīdō, cupīdinis* (f.)
die *morior, morī, mortuus sum*
dig *fodiō, fodere, fōdī, fossum*
direction *regiō, -ōnis* (f.)
discourse *sermō, sermōnis* (m.)
dissolve *solveō, solvēre, solvī, solūtum*
distemper *morbus, -ī* (m.)
ditch *fossa, -ae* (f.)
do *faciō, facere, fēcī, factum*
dog *canis, canis* (m.)
to be done *fīō, fierī, factus sum*
don't ...! *nōlī* ...! *nōlīte* ...!
I don't suppose that ...? *num* ...?
door *porta, -ae* (f.)
down, feathers *plūmae, -ārum* (f.)
draw, drag *trahō, trahere, trāxī, tractum*
draw near *appropinquō, -āre, -āvī, -ātum*
dress *vestiō, vestīre, vestīvī, vestītum*
dung *stercus, stercoris* (n.)

earth *terra, -ae* (f.)
easy *facilis, facile* (gen. *facilis*)
eat *edō, ēsse (edere), ēdī, ēssum (ēsum)*

187

edge *ōra, -ae* (f.)
either ... or ... (not both) *aut ... aut ...*
either ... or ... (or both) *vel ... vel ...*
elevated *celsus, -a, -um*
employer *dominus, -ī* (m.)
enter *introeō, introīre, introīvī, introitum*
entrails *fibra, -ae* (f.)
envoy *lēgātus, -ī* (m.)
equal *pār* (gen. *paris*)
equip *instruō, instruere, instrūxī, instrūctum*
Etruscan *etrūscus, -a, -um*
even, equal *pār* (gen. *paris*)
even, yet *etiam*
every *omnis, omne* (gen. *omnis*)
everybody *omnēs, omnium* (m.)
evildoer *malefactor, -ōris* (m.)
except *nisi* (with the accusative)
exclaim *exclāmō, -āre, -āvī, -ātum*
excrement *stercus, stercoris* (n.)
exhort *hortor, hortārī, hortātus sum*
explain *explicō, -āre, -āvī, -ātum*

face *ōs, ōris* (n.)
face to face, facing *coram* (with the ablative)
a falling *cāsus, -ūs* (m.)
family *genus, generis* (n.); *gēns, gentis* (f.)
famous *celeber, celebris, celebre* (gen. *cēlebris*)
farewell! *valē*!
farmer *agricola, -ae* (m.)
far out! *euge*! *euhoe*!
fashion *modus, -ī* (m.)
fate *fātum, -ī* (n.)
father *pater, patris* (m.)
father-in-law *socer, socerī* (m.)
fatherland *patria, -ae* (f.)

fault *culpa, -ae* (f.)
fear *vereor, verērī, veritus sum*
feather *penna, -ae* (f.); *plūma, -ae* (f.)
featherless *implūmis, implūme* (gen. *implūmis*)
fetter *vinculum, -ī* (n.)
fiber *fibra, -ae* (f.)
field *ager, agrī* (m.)
fierce *rapidus, -a, -um*
fight *pugna, -ae* (f.)
to fight *pugnō, -āre, -āvī, -ātum*
figure out *discō, discere, didicī*
finish *perficiō, perficere, perfēcī, perfectum*
first *prīmus, -a, -um*
first name *praenōmen, -minis* (n.)
fish *piscis, piscis* (m.)
fisherman *piscātor, -ōris* (m.)
fist *pugnum, -ī* (n.)
fit *decōrus, -a, -um; idōneus, -a, -um* (with the dative)
flight *volātus, -ūs* (m.)
fly *volō, -āre, -āvī, -ātum*
fold *plicō, -āre, -āvī, -ātum*
follow *sequor, sequī, secutus sum*
food *cibus, -ī* (m.)
foot *pēs, pedis* (m.)
foot soldier *pedes, peditis* (m.)
for *propter* (with the accusative); *prō* (with the ablative)
for a long time *diū*
for a while longer *diūtius*
foreigner *peregrīnus, -ī* (m.)
forest *silva, -ae* (f.)
forest dwelling *silvāticus, -a, -um*
fork in the road *trivium, -ī* (n.)
former *prior, prius* (gen. *priōris*)
foul *taeter, taetra, taetrum*
(be)fouled *pollūtus, -a, -um*

four-way intersection *quadrivium, -ī* (n.)

fragrant *odōrātus, -a, -um*

France *Gallia, -ae* (f.)

free *līber, lībera, līberum*

to free *solveō, solvēre, solvī, solūtum*

freeze *conglaciō, -āre, -āvī, -ātum*

frequented *celeber, celebris, celebre* (gen. *celebris*)

friend *amīcus, -ī* (m.)

from, out of *ab (ā)* (with the ablative); *ex (ē)* (with the ablative); *dē* (with the ablative)

in front of *prō* (with the ablative)

fruit *pōmum, -ī* (n.)

fruit tree *pōmus, -ī* (m.)

full of glory *gloriōsus, -a, -um*

Gallic *gallicus, -a, -um*

gate *porta, -ae* (f.)

Gaul *Gallia, -ae* (f.)

general *imperātor, -ōris* (m.)

German *germanus, -a, -um*

get down *dēscendō, dēscendere, dēscendi, dēscensum*

girl *puella, -ae* (f.)

give *dō, dare, dedī, datum*

give thanks *grātiās agere*

go! *ī! īte!*

to go *eō, īre, iī, (īvī), itūrus*

go back *redeō, redīre, rediī*

go by *trānscēdō, trānscēdere, trānscessī*

go into *introeō, introīre, introīvī, introitum*

good *bonus, -a, -um*

goodbye! *valē!*

go on foot *ambulō, -āre, -āvī, -ātum*

grandfather *avus, -ī* (m.)

grandmother *avia, -ae* (f.)

great *magnus, -a, -um*

great! *euge! euhoe!*
greed *cupīdō, cupidinis* (f.)
greet *salūto, -āre, -āvi, -ātum*
grow *crescō, crescere, crēvī*
grown°long *prōmissus, -a, -um*
grunt (mil.) *pedes, peditis* (m.)
guard *custōs, custōdis* (m. or f.)
to guard *custōdiō, custōdire, custōdīvī, custōditum*
guilt *culpa, -ae* (f.)

hail! *avē!*
hair *capilla, -ae* (f.)
hand *manus, -ūs* (f.)
hang, cause to be hung *pendō, pendere, pependī, pēnsum*
be happy *gaudeō, gaudēre, gāvisus sum*
as hard as possible *fortissimē*
hat *petasus, -ī* (m.)
haul *trahō, trahere, trāxī, tractum*
have *habeō, habēre, habuī*
he *is; ille; iste; hic*
   he who *quī*
head *caput, capitis* (n.)
hear *audiō, audīre, audīvī, audītum*
heaven *caelum, -ī* (n.)
heavens *sīdera, sīderum* (n.)
hello! *avē! salvē!*
helmsman *gubernātor, -ōris* (m.)
help *auxilium, -ī* (n.)
high *celsus, -a, -um; altus, -a, -um*
himself *ipse; suī*
his own *suus, -a, -um*
hit *feriō, ferīre, ——, ——*
honorific surname *āgnōmen, -minis* (n.)
hooray! *euge!*
horn *cornū, -ūs* (n.)

horse *equus, -ī* (m.)
hour *hōra, -ae* (f.)
house *domus, -ūs (-ī)* (m.)
at the house of *apud* (with the accusative)
how? *quōmodō?*
however *autem*
hunger *famēs, famis* (f.)
hunter *venātor, -ōris* (m.)

I *ego*
if *sī*
if not *nisi* (with the accusative)
impetuous *rapidus, -a, -um*
imprint *imprimō, imprimere, impressī, impressum*
in *in* (with the ablative)
increase *crescō, crescere, crēvī*
indeed *etiam*
infantryman *pedes, peditis* (m.)
inn *taberna, -ae* (f.)
innkeeper *tabernārius, -ī* (m.)
in order that *ut* (with the subjunctive)
instruct *īnstruō, īnstruere, īnstrūxī, īnstructūm*
interjection *interiectiō, -ōnis* (f.)
into *in* (with the accusative)
into the fray *in mediās rēs*
invent *inveniō, invenīre, invēnī, inventum*
island *īnsula, -ae* (f.)
isn't it so that . . . ? *nōnne . . . ?*
it *id; illud; istud; hoc*

javelin *pīlum, -ī* (n.)
journey *iter, itineris* (n.)
to journey *iter facere*
jump *saltō, -āre, -āvī, -ātum*

keeper *custōs, custōdis* (m. or f.)
keep watch *custōdiō, custōdīre, custōdīvī, custōdītum*
kill *interficiō, interficere, interfēcī, interfectum*
king *rēx, rēgis* (m.)
kingdom *rēgnum, -ī* (n.)
knee *genū, genūs* (n.)
know *sapiō, sapere, sapīvī*
knowing, knowledgeable *sapiēns* (gen.) *sapientis*

lack *careō, carēre, caruī, caritūrus*
lamp *lūcerna, -ae* (f.)
lance *pīlum, -ī* (n.)
land *terra, -ae* (f.)
at last *dēnique*
last name *cōgnōmen, -minis* (n.)
last year *priōre annō*
Latin (-speaking) *latīnus, -a, -um*
Latium *Latium, -ī* (n.)
laugh *rīdeō, rīdēre, rīsī, rīsum*
law *lēx, lēgis* (f.)
lawyer *advocātus, -ī* (m.)
lay waste *vastō, -āre, -āvī, -ātum*
lead *agō, agere, ēgī, āctum; dūcō, dūcere, dūxī, dūctum*
leader *dux, ducis* (m.)
leap up *exsiliō, exsilīre, exsiluī*
learn *discō, discere, didicī*
leave *exeō, exīre, exiī, exitum; dēserō, dēserere, dēseruī, dēsertum*
left-hand *sinister, sinistra, sinistrum*
legion *legiō, -ōnis* (f.)
liar *mendāx, mendācis* (m.)
light *lūx, lūcis* (f.)
light-bearing *lūcifer, lūcifera, lūciferum*
lips *ōra, ōrum* (n.); *labia, -ōrum* (n.)
little dog *caniculus, -ī* (m.)
location *locus, -ī* (m.)

lofty *altus, -a, -um*
long for *dēsiderō, -āre, -āvī, -ātum*
look at *aspiciō, aspicere, aspēxī, aspectum*
loosen *solveō, solvēre, soluī, solūtum*
lot *sors, sortis* (f.)
love *amor, amōris* (m.)
to love *amō, -āre, -āvī, -ātum*
low *dēmissus, -a, -um*

be made *fīō, fierī, factus sum*
magistrate *praetor, -ōris* (m.)
make *faciō, facere, fēcī, factum*
make known *nārrō, -āre, -āvī, -ātum*
make one's way *iter facere; iter agere*
make plain *mōnstrō, -āre, -āvī, -ātum*
man *vir, virī* (m.); *homō, hominis* (m.)
march *iter, itineris* (n.)
marketplace *forum, -ī* (n.)
marvelous *mīrābilis, mīrābile* (gen. *mīrābilis*)
masses *vulgus, -ī* (m.)
master (of the house) *dominus, -ī* (m.)
melt away *tābeō, tābēre, ——*
merchant *mercātor, -ōris* (m.)
method *modus, -ī* (m.)
middle *medius, -a, -um*
month *mensis, mensis* (m.)
moon *lūna, -ae* (f.)
moreover *autem*
mother *māter, mātris* (f.)
mouth *ōs, -ōris* (n.)
move *agō, agere, ēgī, āctum*
move back *removeō, removēre, remōvī, remōtum*
murmur, mutter *murmurō, -āre, -āvī, -ātum*
mushroom *fungus, -ī* (m.)
my *meus, -a, -um*

nail *clāvus, -ī* (m.)
name *nōmen, nōminis* (n.)
to name *dēsignō, -āre, -āvī, -ātum*
narrate *nārrō, -āre, -āvī, -ātum*
nature *nātūra, -ae* (f.)
near *prope* (with the accusative)
I need (a body) *opus est mihi* (*corpore*)
neighborhood *vīcīnia, -ae* (f.)
neither (of two) *neuter, neutra, neutrum* (gen. *neutrīus*)
neither ... nor ... *nec ... nec ...*
on the next day *proximō diē*
night *nox, noctis* (f.)
no (way)! *minimē!*
no, none *nūllus, -a, -um* (gen. *nūllīus*)
nobleman *patricius, -ī* (m.)
nobody *nēmō, nūllīus, nemini, neminem, nūllō, -ā, -ō*
noisome *taeter, taetra, taetrum*
not *nōn*
nothing *nihil*
not in the least *minimē*
noun *nōmen, nōminis* (n.)
now *iam; nunc*

oarage *rēmigium, -ī* (n.)
observe *aspiciō, aspicere, aspēxī, aspectum*
occasion for outbreak of war *cāsus bellī*
odd *impār* (gen. *imparis*)
old *antīquus, -a, -um*
on *in* (with the ablative)
one *ūnus, -a, -um* (gen. *ūnīus*)
as one *ūnā*
on the other hand *autem*
... ? or ... ? *utrum ... an ... ?*
... , or not? ... *necne?*
Orcus *Orcus, -ī* (m.)

195

order *imperō, -āre, -āvī, ātum*
in order that *ut* (with the subjunctive)
orchard *pōmārium, -ī* (n.)
other *alter, altera, alterum; alius, alia, aliud* (gen. *alīus*)
our *noster, nostra, nostrum*
outfit *instruō, instruere, instrūxī, instrūctum*
out from *ex (ē)* (with the ablative)
outrageous *immoderātus, -a, -um*
ox *bōs, bovis* (m.)

pain *dolor, dolōris* (m.)
paint *pingō, pingere, pinxī, pictum*
pair *bīnī, bīnae, bīna*
part *pars, partis* (f.)
participle *participium, -ī* (n.)
pass (by) *transcēdō, transcēdere, transcessī*
path *līmes, līmitis* (m.)
patrician *patricius, -ī* (m.)
pear *pirum, ī* (n.)
pear tree *pirus, -ī* (m.)
peg *clāvus, -ī* (m.)
a people *gēns, gentis* (f.)
the people *vulgus, -ī* (m.); *plēbs, plēbis* (f.)
perhaps *forsitan (forsan)*
it is permitted *licet* (with the dative)
perpetuity *perpetuitās, -tātis* (f.)
pick *carpō, carpere, carpsī, carptum*
Pict *pictus, -a, -um*
pig *porcus, -ī* (m.)
pike *vallus, -ī* (m.)
pilgrim *peregrīnus, -ī* (m.)
place *locus, -ī* (m.)
to place *pōnō, pōnere, posuī, positum*
plague *morbus, -ī* (m.)
Plagueville *Morbōnia, -ae* (f.)

pleasant *dulcis, dulce* (gen. *dulcis*)
plebeian *plēbs, plēbis* (f.)
plow *arō, arāre, arāvī, arātum*
poet *poeta, -ae* (m.)
most politely *cōmissimē*
portion *pars, partis* (f.)
praetor *praetor, -ōris* (m.)
prefixing, preposition *praepositiō, ōnis* (f.)
be present *adsum, adesse, adfuī, adfutūrus*
press upon *imprimō, imprimere, impressī, impressum*
pretty *pulcher, pulchra, pulchrum*
price *pretium, -ī* (n.)
high price *caritās, -tātis* (f.)
prior *prior, prius* (gen. *priōris*)
profane *sacer, sacra, sacrum*
pronoun *prōnōmen, -minis* (n.)
public square *forum, -ī* (n.)
put *pōnō, pōnere, posuī, positum*

quaestor *quaestor, -ōris* (m.)

race *gēns, gentis* (f.); *genus, generis* (n.)
rain *imber, imbris* (m.)
rampart *agger, aggeris* (m.)
rare *rārus, -a, -um*
rarely *rārō*
reach *perveniō, pervenīre, pervēnī*
realm *rēgnum, -ī* (n.)
receive *recipiō, recipere, recēpī, receptum*
region *regiō, -ōnis* (f.); *ōra, -ae* (f.)
rejoice *gaudeō, gaudēre, gāvīsus sum*
relaxed *laxus, -a, -um*
remain *maneō, manēre, mānsī*
remove *removeō, removēre, remōvī, remōtum*
resound *resonō, -āre, -āvī, -ātum*

right-hand *dexter, dextera, dexterum*
right on! *euhoe!*
river *flūmen, flūminis* (n.)
road *via, -ae* (f.)
Rome *Rōma, -ae* (f.)
rooster *gallus, -ī* (m.)
rowing apparatus *rēmigium, -ī* (n.)
run *currō, currere, cucurrī, cursum*

sacred *sānctus, -a, -um; sacer, sacra, sacrum*
safe *tutus, -a, -um*
sage *doctus, -a, -um; sapiēns* (gen. *sapientis*)
sailor *nauta, -ae* (m.)
same *īdem, eadem, idem*
sandal *solea, -ae* (f.)
say *dīcō, dīcere, dīxī, dictum; āiō,* etc.; *inquam,* etc.
say farewell *valedīcō, -dīcere, -dīxī*
scarce *rārus, -a, -um*
sea *mare, maris* (n.)
search for *requīrō, requīrere, requīsīvī, requīsītum*
seat *sēdēs, sēdis* (f.)
second *secundus, -a, -um*
see *videō, vidēre, vīdī, vīsum*
seek *requīrō, requīrere, requīsīvī, requīsītum; quaerō, quaerere,
     quaesī, quaesītum*
seemly *decorus, -a, -um*
seize *capiō, capere, cēpī, captum*
seldom *rārō*
self(-same) *ipse, ipsa, ipsum*
sell *vendō, vendere, vendidī,* ——
send *mittō, mittere, mīsī, missum*
send forth *prōmittō, prōmittere, prōmīsī, prōmissum*
servant *famulus, -ī* (m.)
sestertium *sēstertium, -ī* (n.)
several *nōnnūllī, nōnnūllae, nōnnūlla* (gen. *nōnnūllīus*)

shadows *tenebrae, -ārum* (f.)
shake *quatiō, quatere, quassī, quassum*
share *partior, partīrī, partītus sum*
she *ea; illa; ista; haec*
she who *quae*
ship *nāvis, nāvis* (f.)
shoe *calceus, -ī* (m.)
show *mōnstrō, -āre, -āvī, -ātum*
shower (of rain) *imber, imbris* (m.)
Sicily *Sicilia, -ae* (f.)
Sicilians *Siculī, -ōrum* (m.)
sin *reātus, -ūs* (f.)
since *cum; quia*
sit *sedeō, sedēre, sēdī, sessum*
sky *caelum, -ī* (n.)
sky-blue *caeruleus, -a, -um*
sling *funda, -ae* (f.)
small *parvus, -a, -um*
smite *feriō, ferīre, ——*
snake *serpēns, serpentis* (m.)
snatch *carpō, carpere, carpsī, carptum*
snow *nix, nivis* (f.)
soften *molliō, mollīre, mollīvī, mollītum*
soldier *mīles, mīlitis* (m.)
sole *sōlus, -a, -um* (gen. *sōlīus*)
some *nōnnūllus, -a, -um* (gen. *nōnnūllīus*)
somebody *quis*
son *fīlius, -ī* (m.)
sort *genus, generis* (n.)
Spanish *hispānus, -a, -um*
speak of the Devil! *lupus in fābulā!*
speech *sermō, sermōnis* (m.)
more speedily *celerius*
spring forth *exsiliō, exsilīre, exsiluī*
stag *cervus, -ī* (m.)

199

stand *stō, stāre, stetī, statum*
stars *sīdera, sīderum* (n.)
starving *famēlicus, -a, -um*
still, yet *etiam*
stockade *vallum, -ī* (n.)
storekeeper *condus, -ūs* (m.)
story *fābula, -ae* (f.)
stripped *dēnūdātus, -a, -um*
strong *fortis, forte* (gen. *fortis*)
stupid *stultus, -a, -um*
suddenly *subitō*
suitable *idōneus, -a, -um*
summer *aestās, aestātis* (f.)
summon *advocō, -āre, -āvī, -ātum*
sun *sōl, sōlis* (m.)
surname *cōgnōmen, -minis* (n.)
sweet *dulcis, dulce* (gen. *dulcis*)
swift *rapidus, -a, -um*
swine *porcus, -ī* (m.)
sword *gladius, -ī* (m.)

tail *cauda, -ae* (f.)
take up *excipiō, excipere, excēpī, exceptum*
tale *fābula, -ae* (f.)
talking *fābulāns* (gen. *fābulantis*)
taste *sapiō, sapere, sapīvī*
tavern *taberna, -ae* (f.)
tavernkeeper *tabernārius, -ī* (m.)
teach *doceō, docēre, docuī, doctum*
tense *tempus, temporis* (n.)
therefore *ergō*
that (one) *ille, illa, illud*
that one (near you) *iste, ista, istud*
that very (one) *ipse, ipsa, ipsum*
then *tunc*

thing *rēs, reī* (f.)
think *putō, -āre, -āvī, ātum*
third *tertius, -a, -um*
this *hic, haec, hoc*
three *trēs, tria* (gen. *trium*)
three-cornered *triquetrus, -a, -um*
three-way intersection *trivium, -ī* (n.)
through *per* (with the accusative)
throw *iactō, -āre, -āvī, -ātum*
thus *sīc; ita*
time *tempus, temporis* (n.)
to *ad* (with the accusative)
tomorrow *crās*
too *quoque*
torch *fax, facis* (f.)
totality *ūniversitās, -tātis* (f.)
toward *ad* (with the accusative); *in* (with the accusative)
tower *turris, turris* (f.)
trench *fossa, -ae* (f.)
tribune *tribunus, -ī* (m.)
trust *fīdō, fīdere, fīsus sum*
truth *vēritās, -tātis* (f.)
in truth *vērō*
turn (around) *vertō, vertere, vertī, versum*
turtle (-dove) *turtur, turturis* (m.)
two *duo, duae, duo*
two-footed *bipēs* (gen. *bipedis*)
two of a kind *bīnī, bīnae, bīna*

ugly *foedus, -a, -um*
under *sub* (with the ablative)
Underworld *Orcus, -ī* (m.); *Ōrae Acheruntis, Ōrārum Acheruntis* (f.)
unequal, uneven *impār* (gen. *imparis*)
unfold *explicō, -āre, -āvī, -ātum*
unhappy *īnfēlix* (gen. *īnfēlīcis*)

universe, university *ūniversitās, -tātis* (f.)
unrestrained *laxus, -a, -um; immoderātus, -a, -um*
urge *hortor, hortārī, hortātus sum*

vanish *ēvānescō, ēvānescere, ēvānuī*
verb *verbum, -ī* (n.)
very much *nimis*
very *very* much *nimius*
Vesuvius *Vesuvius, -ī* (m.)
vicinity *vīcīnia, -ae* (f.)
Visigoth *visigothus, -a, -um*
voice *vox, vōcis* (f.)

walk *ambulō, -āre, -āvī, -ātum*
wall *mūrus, -ī* (m.)
walled town *urbs, urbis* (f.)
want *dēsiderō, -āre, -āvī, -ātum; volō, velle, voluī*
war *bellum, -ī* (n.)
warn *moneō, monēre, monuī, monitum*
waste (mil.) *vastō, -āre, -āvī, -ātum*
waste away *tābeō, tābēre,* ——
water *aqua, -ae* (f.)
water clock *clepsydra, -ae* (f.)
wave *unda, -ae* (f.)
wax *cēra, -ae* (f.)
way (road) *via, -ae* (f.); *iter, itineris* (n.)
way (method) *modus, -ī* (m.)
we *nōs, nostrum (nostrī)*
wearing a hat *petasātus, -a, -um*
weigh down *gravō, -āre, -āvī, -ātum*
when *quandō; cum*
whence *unde*
where *ubi*
where from *unde*
where to *quō*

that which ... *quod* ...

which (of two) *uter, utra, utrum* (gen. *utrīus*)

white *albus, -a, -um*

whither *quō*

who ... ? *quis* ... ?

(he) who ... *quī* ...

whoever *quis*

whole *tōtus, -a, -um* (gen. *tōtīus*)

why? *quārē?*

wild *silvāticus, -a, -um*

window *fenestra, -ae* (f.)

winter *hiems, hiemis* (f.)

wish *dēsīderō, -āre, -āvī, -ātum; volō, velle, voluī*

wish not *nōlō, nōlle, nōluī*

with *cum* (with the ablative); *apud* (with the accusative)

withdraw *removeō, removēre, remōvī, remōtum*

without *sine* (with the ablative)

wolf *lupus, -ī* (m.)

wonderful *mīrus, -a, -um*

word *verbum, -ī* (n.)

world *mundus, -ī* (m.)

would that *ut* (with the subjunctive); *utinam* (with the subjunctive)

write *scrībō, scrībere, scrīpsī, scrīptum*

year *annus, -ī* (m.)

yes *certē; vērō; sīc; ita*

yesterday *herī*

yet *etiam*

you (sing.) *tū, tuī;* (pl.) *vōs, vestrum, vestrī*)

your (sing.) *tuus, -a, -um;* (pl.) *vester, vestra, vestrum*

We would like to express our gratitude to family and friends for their indispensable assistance in bringing this book to life.

To our family first: the role of Euhemerus is played by our great-grandfather, C. W. Gleason; that of mother and father, by our parents, David E. Humez and Elisabeth Gleason Humez, who were not only kind enough to beget us, care for us, and illuminate many of our darker corners, but also thought to acquaint us with most of the shaggy dog stories in this book; gentle reader, tactful critic, and boon companion: Jean McMahon Humez.

Classic mentors and excellent guides: Warren Cowgill, Howard Garey, Alfred Geier, Paul Hennessey, Stanley Insler, Ralph MacElearney, Demetrios Moutsos, and the late Kenneth Rose.

Neo-Classic mentors and excellent guides: Llewellyn Howland III, whose idea we hope was something like this; and Luise Erdmann, a patient and diplomatic person if ever there was one.

General encouragement and egging on (profusely illustrated): Rufus Chaffee, Ross Faneuf, and Howard Morgan (and a supporting cast of unspecified but grandiose number).

We would also like to thank the people who make the Boston Athenaeum, the rare book room of the Boston Public Library, the Cambridge Public Library, and the Houghton Library of Harvard University the terrific resources that they are. These institutions have graciously provided the illustrations that appear in this book.

Index

205